A Steady Stream of Praise for Peeing in Peace . . .

"For all the working moms who feel like they are about to drop the balls they've been juggling (i.e., all of us!), take heart. *Peeing in Peace* is filled with humor, compassion, and sage advice. I only wish Beth and Yvette had been around when my daughters were younger. Make time to read this book, even if you have to lock yourself in the bathroom."

—Arianna Huffington, author of
   On Becoming Fearless

"Like that euphoric feeling when you walk through the door of your home for the first time, *Peeing in Peace* welcomes working moms with open arms, awesome advice, and pee in your pants moments. A must read for any mom who needs a little boost while trying to juggle business and babies."

—Barbara Corcoran, real estate mogul
   and author

"From the adorable cover to the laugh-out-loud chapters to the priceless parenting tips — *Peeing in Peace* had me smiling from start to finish."

—Marg Helgenberger, *CSI* television
    star and feature film actress

"If you've ever soaped up with the shower door open so you can watch the baby at the same time, piled furniture to build a "demilitarized zone" between your kids, or looked forward to Mondays because your high-powered job is comparatively restful, this is the book for you! Yvette Corporon and Beth Feldman have penned a laugh-out-loud rendition of parenting that will inspire you and give you strength for the next birthday party, middle of the night ER trip, or burping-decorated business suit. Full of wisdom on loving both your work and your kids like crazy."

—Donna Hanover, host,
    WOR Radio *Morning Show*

"Like a much-needed coffee break with your best girlfriends, *Peeing in Peace* is the perfect remedy for overwhelmed moms.

Corporon and Feldman write from the heart, with humor and rueful recognition of the sacrifices working moms have to make, while rejoicing in the rewards, big and small, of raising children."

—Melanie Lynne Hauser, author
of *Confessions of Super Mom*

"Balance is a demanding mistress who often sleeps alone. But knowing you're not alone is worth its weight in comedy gold. Read it, laugh through it, and for God's sake, buy it!"

—Eva LaRue, *CSI: Miami* television star
and feature film actress

"Thanks to Beth and Yvette for this hilarious, startlingly candid working-mom manifesto. Every mother can identify with their deliciously vivid laugh-out-loud recounts of minivan-to-boardroom moments. The authors have beautifully and tenderly captured the complex push-pull inherent in being a power-mommy."

—Sabrina Weill, editor in chief, Mom Logic, and author, *The Real Truth about Teens and Sex*

"I truly enjoyed this book!! It was a laugh-out-loud read and I was nodding my head in agreement while reading. Beth and Yvette should both be so proud of what they've accomplished. I wanted more when it was over!!"

—Alexis Christoforous, CBS *Marketwatch* anchor

"Whether you have children or not . . . [readers] have a connection with stories like yours. I love the play-date stuff . . . and the children's parties. I have nine nieces and nephews, plus my closest friends from high school all have kids (and they were and some still are working moms) . . . so I know some of the horror stories about these things that have become a part of our culture. CONGRATULATIONS on the book . . . you did a beautiful job!!!"

—Linda Schmidt, news reporter, WNYW FOX 5 TV, New York

"With candor, intelligence, and humor to spare, *Peeing in Peace* should be tucked into every mom's purse—and diaper bag! With a nonjudgmental voice, Beth and Yvette's personal tales are conveyed in a way that regardless of whether you are a working mom, working from home mom, or headquartered out of your home working AS a mom, you will smile and see glimpses of your own maternal experience.

An equally perfect gift for the new mommy who's heading back to the office or the one who has decided to 'stay home,' the giggles provoked by *Peeing in Peace* can ease the toughest of Mommy transitions. I highly recommend it!"

—Cheryl Lage, author of *Twinspiration*

"Busy working moms will want to stash this funny little book in their purses for moments of support, from the creators of rolemommy.com."

—*OK! Magazine*

Peeing in Peace

Tales and Tips for Type A Moms

Beth Feldman & Yvette Manessis Corporon

SOURCEBOOKS, INC.®
NAPERVILLE, ILLINOIS

Published by Sourcebooks, Inc.
P.O. Box 4410, Naperville, Illinois 60567-4410
(630) 961-3900
Fax: (630) 961-2168
www.sourcebooks.com

Originally published in 2007 by NK Publications

Library of Congress Cataloging-in-Publication Data

Feldman, Beth.
  Peeing in peace : tales and tips for Type A moms / Beth Feldman and Yvette Manessis
Corporon.
    p. cm.
  1. Mothers. 2. Motherhood–Humor. 3. Parenting–Humor. I. Corporon, Yvette Manessis. II.
Title.
HQ759.F34 2008
306.874'3–dc22

                             2007049268

                         Printed in Canada
                     WC 10 9 8 7 6 5 4 3 2 1

Contents

Dedication

FOR OUR children—Rebecca and Dylan and Christiana and Nico. Now you know why mommy needed the computer and wouldn't let you log on to NickJr.com. Every day you amaze and inspire us to be better moms. Thanks for all the great material and making us laugh out loud even when we are having a Mommy Dearest moment. We love you. Now, stop stalling and go to bed.

Introduction

Before We Begin

IF YOU'RE like most new mothers who have recently returned to work, there are two questions keeping you awake at night along with your baby. How am I going to do this? Where do I fit in?

As you try to strike a balance between two very demanding worlds without losing your job, your husband, your time with your children, or your sanity, allow us to introduce you to our version of the mother's little helper.

Welcome to where you finally fit in. Welcome to *Peeing in Peace*—the perfect playdate for your purse. Between the pages of this book, you will find your community, your confidantes, and, oftentimes, coconspirators.

Since we're going to be spending some quality time together, allow us to introduce ourselves. We are Beth Feldman and Yvette Corporon, two working mothers who are the creators of Role Mommy, www.rolemommy. com, an online community and virtual coffee klatch for today's busy moms.

"What is a Role Mommy?" you ask. If you never thought you were a role model, think again. We believe that every working mother is a role model for other working moms. She's an inspiration, a source of advice, a springboard for ideas, a confidante to laugh with, and a reality check to remind us that we are certainly not alone.

Remember, there's strength in numbers, and if we just stick together, there isn't a diaper, dilemma, or deadline we can't overcome. So put the kids to bed, grab a glass of wine, enjoy the quiet, and dive in.

OUR LIVES...

B.C. before children
and
after diapers A.D.

Afternoon Delight

B.C. About 3 p.m. on a rainy Sunday afternoon. You and your boyfriend, lover, whatever, roll over lazily and enjoy another roll in the hay. You then walk buck naked to the kitchen and pour yourselves yet another round of Bloody Marys before reading the *New York Times* cover to cover.

A.D. About 3 p.m. on a rainy Sunday afternoon when your colicky baby, who's been up since 5 a.m., finally goes down for a nap while your preschooler is at her friend's house for a playdate. You and your husband excitedly race to the bedroom, close the blinds, unplug the phone, jump into bed, and have the most intense, satisfying, and earth shattering nap either one of you have ever experienced.

1

Peeing in Peace

ADMIT IT. As much as you look forward to Fridays, to finally having the weekend home with your family, sometimes you look forward to Mondays even more.

Who can blame you? Certainly not us. After a long exhausting weekend, running to the cleaners, ballet class, baseball practice, the pediatrician, the post office, and every birthday party from power rangers to princess—isn't it nice to finally get back to the office and pee in peace? There, you can relish relieving yourself in private—nobody banging on the bathroom door to get in, and no toddler demanding to sit on your lap as you try to tinkle.

You know you're a working mom when you sometimes go to the office to relax.

It's not that you don't love the time you spend with your family. But after playing short-order cook to some of the pickiest eaters on the planet, answering the same question for the umpteenth time in one day, and trying to reason with a two-year-old who is singing "Old MacDonald" one minute and throwing a hissy fit in the checkout line of the supermarket the next, isn't it nice to get back to the office and make that amazing transformation from mommy to mogul?

Back at work, you don't have to explain to your boss why eating fruit roll-ups every day of the week will inevitably rot your teeth. And although you may be kissing a lot of butt on the job, at least you're not wiping it.

Think back to those last few days of your precious maternity leave: bleary-eyed from lack of sleep, boobs on fire from breastfeeding, and terrified by the prospect of leaving your helpless baby at home. Finally, the day arrives and you reluctantly head back to work. Leaving home that first morning is pure hell. You ride to the office wondering how you'll ever survive being away from your beautiful baby. You arrive, a teary, emotional wreck. Between checking email, showing off your baby brag book, and catching up with colleagues, you call home at least a dozen times that morning. Your frustrated yet patient baby-sitter assures you that nothing's changed since you last called 10 minutes ago and, yes, the baby is still breathing. Satisfied—for at least a few more minutes anyway—you head out to get some lunch. That's when it hits you.

You can eat. You can actually sit at a table like a regular human being and, rather than lap up last night's leftovers or nibble on some chicken nuggets from a half-eaten Happy Meal, you can order that tuna sashimi you've been craving since the day you first found out you were pregnant. No spit-up to clean, no dirty diapers to change, no bottles to wash, no crying to comfort, and nobody clinging to you as you try in vain to take a bite. You quickly realize, hey, this isn't so bad after all. You kind of like going to work.

Oh, but it doesn't end with the ladies room or lunch. There's so much more to love.

The Cinderella Syndrome

IN FACT, the commute can be your very own coach ride to Cinderella's ball. We call it the Cinderella Syndrome. No matter your mode of transport, on the way to work your meta-morphosis begins. With no one fighting over who had what first and the sweet sounds of silence drowning out the fading echoes of "Mommy, mommy, mommy, mommy, mommy," you give yourself just enough time to purchase a newspaper and the breakfast of champions—sugar free vanilla skim latte, or a Coffee Coolata if Dunkin Donuts is your guilty pleasure. For some of us, the chance to be alone in our car, listening to anything but the soundtrack to *High School Musical* or "Baby Beluga" is pure paradise.

On the road, you can relax, refresh, and maybe even have time for a little red light rejuvenation, where you slap on as much makeup as you can before the light turns green again. Yes, it's true: lip gloss does indeed have healing powers.

You arrive at the office, the modern mom's version of the fairy tale ball. You spend the day searching for Prince Charming (a boss who won't bat an eye when you show up at 11 a.m.) and sparring with the wicked stepsisters—(the bean counters in finance who don't think your baby-sitter's overtime is a billable expense). As tough as your day may be sometimes, the magic is still there. Here, at the office, you are seen as more than someone's mom, more than a carpool queen, more than a walking coat rack for your kids, and more than the woman who's blacklisted at Blockbuster because she owes $76 from overdue and lost videos.

Here, at the office, you are seen as a woman with a brain.

But as the clock strikes 5 p.m. the spell begins to fade. You get back on the road, and with every mile, you once again morph back into mommy. It's bye-bye to the brainiac and hello to the little maniacs who are waiting in the window as you pull up to your home. Their deafening screams and giggles are even sweeter because you know that your silent coach will once again await you at 8 a.m. tomorrow morning.

Baby Talk

AFTER YOU'VE enjoyed the golden silence of your commute to work comes the unexpected pleasure of a little adult conversation. If you've never thought putting more than two syllables together could be rewarding, we guarantee you haven't been a new mother. The most highly educated woman will tell you that try as you might, you can't help but be reduced to a blithering idiot when you babble baby talk while gazing lovingly at your infant. Even if you've managed to avoid the cliché goo-goos and ga-gas, we guarantee you've repeated dada and mama at least a million times in an effort to get your utterly adorable infant to utter her first words.

As your baby becomes more mobile, you become a master of monosyllabic commands. Full sentences go out the window when your baby is inching her way toward disaster. Time is of the essence because those little limbs are moving at lightning speed, and there's no time to waste with unnecessary words. "Be careful, the stove is hot," quickly becomes "HOT" and "Please don't touch mommy's manuscript, her entire career is riding on it," easily translates to "NOOOOOO!" It's virtually impossible to explain to someone the joys of speaking in full sentences again unless you've spent time in this language limbo.

In the office, from your first "Good morning, how are you today?" to your last "Have those reports on my desk at 9 a.m., or else," it's an absolute pleasure to use that atrophying part of your brain and savor a little adult conversation. It's not that you don't care if Dora and Diego save baby leopard from the roaring rapids, it's just nice to spend the morning saying more than "Swiper, no Swiping."

Code Word: Gotta Go!

THIS PHRASE takes on two different meanings when you're a busy mom. First up, the "GOTTA GO" that's said every time your child has to hit the potty. There's nothing like a three-year-old who thinks she has to tinkle every time you're in line at Costco and you finally have the cash register in sight to make you long for the good old days of diapers.

The second, "GOTTA GO" we're referring to, is the one that gets you crazy every time you try to talk on the phone when you're at home. Before we had kids, we could ring up our own personal posse without a problem—we'd catch up with our girlfriends, boyfriends, fake friends, check in with mom, and even call our old boyfriends and hang up when they answered (those were the good old days before caller ID made stalking virtually impossible).

Unfortunately, the days of spending endless hours gabbing away in our very own gossip fest are far behind us. Today, if the telephone rings and your children are in earshot, be sure that within the first 17 seconds of your call, your child will call out your name.

Then, they will scream it.

Then, they will pick a fight with their brothers and sisters.

Then, they will scream your name again, LOUDER.

If you don't take the bait, one of them will inevitably find you (usually the younger one), wave a Costume Express catalog in your face, grab you by the hand, escort you to your computer, and force you to log onto their website and place an order for an overpriced superhero outfit that they don't really need (because they already phone-jacked you a month earlier to make a similar purchase while you were trying to have a meaningful conversation with your mother-in-law).

As mothers, we all occasionally come down with a case of the "GOTTA GO's." That's when the phone rings and you walk into another room hopelessly trying to ignore your kids' attention-seeking sabotages. Inevitably, you hear a loud crash, which is usually followed by a scream or a cry and sometimes both. It is at this moment that the code is called into action. "GOTTA GO." Translation: "I'll call you back when I'm at work so we can catch up."

If you're suffering from a case of the "GOTTA GO's," then your workplace becomes the perfect hideout to finally finish all those fragmented phone calls. We're not saying stay on the line for hours on end—you are on company time. But take advantage of your environment and enjoy a little uninterrupted talking. Seriously, if you don't do it for yourself, at least do it for all your frustrated friends who are constantly being cut off mid-sentence. It's bad enough listening to your own kids scream, think of your poor friends who call to chat and end up with an earful of a five-year-old fighting with their younger brother while you fumble for contraband snacks just to keep them quiet.

So, the next time your phone rings and your son sees it as a signal to grab the step ladder and pull down his Halloween stash, save yourself a headache and a chunk of change on those dentist bills. Simply say "GOTTA GO—I'll call you from the office," and hand that little conniver some carrots.

It's Not Easy Being Clean . . .

IF THAT'S not enough reason to love work, think about the basic necessities, such as human hygiene. Recall those early days of motherhood when your only goal for the day was to take a shower. You'd make a bold attempt, buckling your newborn into his or her bouncy seat, flipping on "Baby Einstein," and hoping that your tiny bundle of joy would be entertained by a sock puppet who shouted "Blech" every 10 seconds. But nine times out of ten, your baby would launch into hysterics and you'd wind up hitting the sheets that night exhausted and still smelly. As children enter their toddler years, showering for some of us becomes a spectator sport—with our tykes sitting on the bathroom floor, staring at us while we try to steal a nanosecond of privacy. When your little one starts shouting, "Mommy has a big butt," it's time to draw the line: pull that shower curtain shut and invest in a new DVD collection.

Now that you're back at work, you have to shower—it's no longer a luxury; it's a requirement. So even if it's a 60-second sponge bath with the door open and one eye on the kids as they play battleship in the bidet, as long as you get in a shampoo and a shave, you're golden.

Give Up the Guilt!

FOR THOSE of you still wrestling with the guilt, we're here to let you in on a little secret. There is nothing wrong with admitting that you like to go to work. We know you miss your kids; we do, too. You love your kids—but it's okay to love your career, too.

Whereas we spend endless hours catering to the needs and whims of our children, we sometimes forget that our jobs were our first babies. Much like our kids, we nurtured our careers and watched them grow. Now, it's amazing to look back and see how much like our children our careers really are. We all know how much a cranky client and a colicky baby have in common. Both can be unreasonable, act inconsolable, and keep you up all night with their demands.

But after a long day negotiating, troubleshooting, and Power Pointing at the office, the multitasking mama that you are can head home to comfort, coddle, and clean the sticky fingered munchkins who greet you at the door, serenading you with a *Sound of Music*- worthy chorus of "Mommy's home." No matter how tired or tense you are from the demands of your job, everything else falls away as your children fall into your arms.

Role Mommy
Reality Check

There is nothing that can ever compare to that feeling when you finally hug your kids at the end of a busy day. No promotion, raise, or amazing new job offer will ever compete. But let's face it . . . sometimes peeing in peace can come pretty close.

OUR LIVES...
B.C. before children
and
after diapers A.D.

Conference Calls

B.C. Those extremely productive phone calls, where several bright, eloquent, and successful professionals come together to share ideas, exchange information, and ask for your input and opinions on making important business decisions.

A.D. Those maddening telephone conversations, where your children are screaming in the background as you simultaneously speak on your cell phone and office phone and type away on your PDA and desktop, while also trying to arrange your child's playdates, carpool, and soccer schedule. Tip: The mute button works extremely well in these situations.

2

Corporate Chutes & Ladders

DO YOU remember the time when your career was the most important thing in your life? You happily worked eighteen-hour days, took on every project that was thrown in your direction, jumped at the chance to take on more responsibility, and went on any and every business trip everyone else in your office just couldn't be bothered with. You were the "go-to" girl—the up and comer with all the answers and boundless energy.

After years of proving yourself, pulling off the impossible, and fighting off every

idea-stealing leech in the office, you finally
clawed your way up the corporate ladder.
Congratulations. So, here you are, at the top
of your game.

Enter baby. Now what do you do?

Welcome to the world of Corporate Chutes
and Ladders. It's the game that challenges
working moms to keep a firm grasp on the
corporate ladder and, if they're really brave,
continue climbing. But now, with briefcase
and baby on board, the rules have changed,
and things are trickier than ever.

In this game, the ladder is now greased
with diaper ointment and SPF 45 sunblock.
There are no "get out of jail free" cards to play
when your teething baby decides to pull an all-
nighter the night before your big presentation.
You're still playing against the leeches, but now
they're even hungrier than before. They're
pissed off they were passed over for that last
promotion, they're out for your job, and they
can smell maternal conflict a mile away.

The goal of this game is to make it through
the working mother gauntlet. You must master
the art of multitasking—survive sneak attacks
and sabotage attempts by the leeches, find a

way to make an appearance at "Preschool Teacher Appreciation Day," get to work on time, pull off your presentation flawlessly, and still make it home before your children are already asleep.

There are a million ways to play this game. Some women just keep on climbing higher and higher up that ladder, never missing a beat and barely even pausing long enough to give birth. Others take some time off, step off the ladder, and decide they want to trade in their MBA for midday Mommy and Me Yoga classes.

Then, there are the rest of us, the majority of working moms who struggle with Corporate Chutes and Ladders every single day of our lives. Sometimes we take a few steps forward. After all, we're still the same brilliant women we were before babies came into our lives. But let's face it, every now and then we slip a bit . . . our baby-sitters show up late and our carefully structured house of cards comes tumbling down.

One word of warning: Don't believe everything you read. As tough as it may be sometimes to balance it all, we're not conflicted. Contrary to all those condescending headlines and magazine articles, there is no debate for us. We have jobs and we have children. We want them both to grow and thrive.

We want to run the company, but we also want to be the ones our kids run to when they need a hug. We want to read about ourselves in the company newsletter, but we also want to read our kids bedtime stories at the end of the day. We want to follow our hearts and do what we love, but we know that ultimately our hearts will always lead us home to the people we love.

Having children didn't quench our desire to race up that damn ladder and break through the glass ceiling. For some of us, all it did was alter our course a bit . . . some chutes, some ladders, but we'll still get there. The difference is that having children changed the timeline a bit.

Climbing the Ladder with the Goddess of Good Morning America
Yvette's Story

I HAVE always idolized Diane Sawyer. To me, this beautiful, smart, and elegant woman embodies everything I've always aspired to be. She can grill President Bush with the greatest of ease and then, without missing a beat or a page of her script, move effortlessly on to an interview with a scandal-plagued starlet. And she always injects personality and humor and oozes elegance and intelligence with every word, not to mention she wears that halo of perfectly coiffed blonde hair, strategically placed just so over her eye. The woman is quite simply a television news goddess.

While I was working as a freelance television producer, I was offered a job at *Good Morning America*. My daughter, Christiana, was about seven months old at the time, and although I knew the job would mean long hours away from my little love, I jumped at the chance to work with my idol.

Professionally, I was in heaven. Working for *Good Morning America* was the proverbial dream come true. Writing for Diane, Charlie Gibson, and Robin Roberts was truly the most rewarding time of my career. I was scared to death I would screw it up. Every time I walked in through the security desk in the morning, coffee in hand, I would flash my ID card and wait for the day when someone would catch on, call me a hoax, and have me escorted from the building.

I had stress knots in my stomach every time I handed in a script. Would they hate it, finally figure out that I didn't know how to write, or maybe, if my script was even worse than I suspected, would they think I was a ringer sent in by the other morning shows to mess with the competition?

Lucky for me, they never caught on. I stayed—in a big windowed office at ABC News.

I was overjoyed to hear my words, my carefully chosen double entendres, and my oh-so-eloquent alliteration coming out of Diane's, Charlie's, and Robin's mouths. I was living the dream, or so it seemed.

There I was in my network news office, doing what I loved for people I respected and admired. Why was I so miserable?

I missed my baby.

There were so many late nights spent writing, rewriting, editing, and re-editing— holidays, weekends, and all hours of the day and night.

At work, I was progressing up the ladder. At home, I felt Christiana's infancy was slipping away and I was missing it.

I looked around me at all the amazing women that I was working with. How did they do it? What was their secret? I quickly realized that there was no secret. There are choices.

There were women who chose to hire around-the-clock help. They had their day nanny, their night nanny, and a weekend nanny on call in case they were called out of town on breaking news. There were women whose husbands stayed home or had jobs that allowed them the flexibility to spend more time at home taking care of the kids. There were women whose children were a bit older—who could be picked up from school and hang out in mom's office doing homework while she finished up for the day. Then, there was me.

As much as I wanted network news success, I wasn't willing to sacrifice Christiana's infancy in exchange.

After a few months of living out my dream, I decided it was time to go back home to my baby and my life as a freelancer. I would be free to pick and choose my projects and control exactly how much time I spent away from home. Some may see my decision to leave *Good Morning America* and go back to freelancing as slipping a few rungs down the corporate ladder. I don't. I see it as a way to stay on the ladder while watching my baby grow.

Today, I'm back at work full time as a producer for the entertainment news show *Extra*. I'm still doing what I love, but now I'm covering celebrities and getting home almost every night to put my kids to bed.

Every now and then I get to revisit my idols at *Good Morning America*. Only now I'm on the other side of Diane's microphone. I head over to the *GMA* studio to interview Diane about her latest A-list "get" or the huge news story of the day. Every time I walk through those doors and on to the *GMA* set, I have a twinge of "what if?" What if I would have stayed? I might have been the producer traveling to North Korea with Diane. I might have been the one sitting down in the White House with President Bush to drill him on the crisis in the Middle East. What if I had stayed on course and followed my dream of a network news career? What if? What if?

Finally, for the first time in my life I feel the answers outweigh the questions. The most rewarding and precious moments in my life haven't been spent in a newsroom, in a studio, out in the field, or even up on stage accepting my Emmy award. They were spent in my bathtub and my bed—splashing and cuddling with my children.

Maybe one day I'll reclaim my network career, my big windowed office at ABC News, and the permanent stress knot that seemed to accompany it. But for now, I'm happy to stay right where I am. My feet are planted firmly on the ladder, and my arms are firmly around my children.

Staying in the Game

Beth's Story

I BECAME a career gal with the theme song to *Working Girl* blaring in my head. My "never give up" attitude has always been a part of my genetic makeup, so when I became pregnant with my daughter, I knew that I would go back to work fulltime. Sure I took a few months off, but it wasn't my style to jump off the ladder and take a chance on the hope that someone would still hire me on a part-time basis. "Slow and steady, stay with what you know"—that was my mantra. And what I knew at the time was that I had some forward-thinking bosses who might just go for the scenario I was concocting in my head while my baby was growing in my belly.

Would they consider allowing me to tele-commute two days a week so that I could see my infant take her first steps or babble her first words during the morning hours and not after a long day in the office? I'd still be working, but at least I'd be nearby if anything exciting or catastrophic happened that day in my bustling home.

As luck would have it, they gave me a six-week tryout, and telecommuting worked like a charm. So much so, that after six years and the birth of my son, I've become the telecom-muting pioneer for other working moms in my department who've been given the chance to work from home so they can get a slice of the quality-of-life pie, too.

Although this wonderful opportunity has been a blessing, it has also played a role in making my climb up the ladder more like the long and winding road. I enviously watched as my peers with five-day-a-week work schedules moved up quickly, rung by rung, in the express lane, while I was reduced to taking the slower carpool route.

Throughout my career, I have always been the go-getter. If there was a choice assignment, I'd be first in line to ask for it. I've launched more television series than I care to recount—spending countless hours freezing and famished outside of an actor's trailer waiting for him to grant an interview. I've raced across Nashville, nabbing exclusive interviews with chart-topping music stars, and have nibbled on the veggie and cookie platters in every green room from Regis to Letterman to Oprah. I've somehow managed to convince eager and agreeable actors to participate in pizza tastings, drag races, and salacious celebrity roasts, and I even forced one actor of a failing sitcom to pose in the window of a Bed, Bath & Beyond store so that I could get Yvette to send a camera crew to cover it.

But despite loving the glitz, glamour, and outrageous stunts, the stress of those early

mornings—where I'd frantically wait by my
front door for my baby-sitter to arrive so I could
catch the 7:02 train—was making me a nervous
wreck. Add to that the pressure of spending
twelve-hour days on the set of a sitcom whose
ratings were in the dumpster and the time an
irrational actress screamed at me at a photo
shoot while I was nine months pregnant—I
had finally reached my boiling point.

Three days later, when the demands of my
life sent me into premature labor and I was
busy firing off emails between my contrac-
tions so my assistant could take care of all
the loose ends that I thought I could manage
before my due date, I decided it was time for
a change.

Although I loved my job and didn't want
to quit, I knew it was time for a career adjust-
ment so I could truly accommodate the work/
life balance I had set in motion when my
daughter was born. I crafted another proposal
to my boss, this time devising a new posi-
tion, where I could finally move out of the
trenches and into the land of the corporate
big picture. Lucky for me, he was impressed
by the pitch.

After playing several rounds of the waiting game, I've finally made it to the top of my ladder. I thought I'd find all the answers once I broke through the glass ceiling, but I've realized I won't be content to just sit here picking shrapnel off my suit. That's the funny thing about the corporate ladder. Once you finally reach the top, you want to either keep climbing higher or jump off completely to tackle something new.

Role Mommy
Reality Check

Contrary to popular belief, having it all is not some unattainable urban legend or a mommy myth. It really is possible. The key is realizing that having it all means different things at different stages in your life. When it comes to your career, there's nothing wrong with taking a baby-induced detour or staying on the train and moving full steam ahead. Sometimes the smartest business advice is to simply trust your instincts and follow your passion. In the end, the choices you make along your journey will ultimately guide you to exactly where you want to be.

B.C. before children
and
after diapers A.D.

Business Lunch

B.C. You sat in a restaurant and were waited upon and served appetizers, entrees, and dessert as you discussed work with a colleague or client.

A.D. You spend your lunch hour running around town like a lunatic as you take care of all your family's needs—hitting the post office, the pharmacy, the dry cleaners, and Old Navy—before racing back to the office, where you scarf down a Balance Bar at your desk and call it lunch while trolling through eBay to find the out-of-stock American Girl doll your daughter just has to get her little hands on.

3

What Color Is Your Pantyhose?

WHEN YOU first jumped into the job market, you may have read the career-building bible *What Color is Your Parachute?*—an instructional guide that helps you pinpoint the career that is best for you and your unique talents. Since choosing your profession, you charged ahead earning promotion after promotion until baby number one came along. Then, suddenly you hit a standstill. Now that you have to dash out before everyone else to pick up your child from daycare, your career prospects seem to have stalled, just as your clothes have tightened. Have you lost the steam to move ahead?

It's time for a stress-free quiz on the state of your life. It's called "What Color Is Your Pantyhose?" and as you will soon find out, what you're wearing says a lot about where you're headed at this stage of the game.

Let's start with our pop quiz.

Hose in the Office . . .

1. PASSED OVER FOR A PROMOTION

Q. Your boss has just passed you over for a promotion, due in part to your flexible work schedule. You're infuriated because you can accomplish more in three 8-hour days than that newly promoted sycophant can accomplish in five 12-hour days. The adrenaline is flowing and you decide to:

- A. Draft a convincing Power Point presentation illustrating why you should be promoted, too.
- B. March into your boss's office while he's in the middle of an important meeting with the auditors. Without warning, you let him have it as the accounting crew

stares at you in exasperation. Your boss, whose face is now the color of a turnip, immediately kicks you out and puts a little red mark next to your name.

C. Complain about the injustice to your boss's assistant, the mailroom guy, your best friend, and your fellow coworkers, but you do absolutely nothing else about it.

D. Go to that facial appointment you made prior to your boss dropping the bomb on you.

2. MULTITASKING CONUNDRUM

You have a 3:30 p.m. meeting with the top brass, but your nanny just called to tell you that your three-year-old is running a high fever and you need to get her to the doctor. You:

A. Call the doctor, get the last appointment of the day, go to your meeting, sound brilliant (all the while worrying about your sick child), and race out the door to catch the train, pick up your daughter, and get her to the pediatrician before they lock up.

    B. Call your husband and demand that he race home to pick up your child and take her to the doctor. When he says he can't do it, you lose it, start crying, and make him feel guilty, and he changes his mind, packs up his things, and heads home to tend to your child.

    C. Consult five different working moms in the office who suggest that you tell your baby-sitter to give your child a Tylenol and head home right after your meeting.

    D. Tell your bosses you can't make the meeting, pick up your daughter, and get to the doctor's office in record time.

Hose at Home

1. SPORTS NUT

Your child has just handed you a long list of school teams that he'd like to join. You . . .

    A. Tell him to pick two activities, sign him up, and make sure you're on hand to watch from the sidelines whenever you can.

    B. Don't pay attention to what he's asking, "yes" him to death, and then get really annoyed when you realize you have to fork over $500 for team uniforms and sell twenty boxes of super-sized M&M's.

C. Tell him he can sign up for everything on the list and then desperately search for ways you're going to get him to and from all those practices.

D. Promise to sign him up for football and soccer but then forget to mail the form on time, and your son winds up crocheting pot holders at the only class that's still left open: Art from the Heart.

2. CARPOOL CONUNDRUM

Your daughter has begged and pleaded that you enroll her in Girl Scouts, but here's your problem: the meetings are held when you're in the office, and you need to figure out how you're going to transport her to her weekly powwow.

A. You make sure your daughter will be in a troop with your friend's child and ask if she will handle pick-up duties while you're at work. You then promise that you'll repay the favor by personally selling her daughter's stash of cookies to all of your unsuspecting coworkers. Besides, who doesn't like a good Girl Scout Samoa every now and again?

B. You begrudgingly sign your daughter up for Scouts, but no one wants to be in your carpool because of your short fuse and the fact that you probably won't be able to pitch in with carpool duty anyway.

C. Anything for your little princess. You sign her up, join three carpools, and then over-extend yourself and have to leave early every other week because it's your turn to run the Girl Scout shuttle.

D. You tell your daughter you'll sign her up, you forget to mail in the form, and the next thing you know, your child is front and center at Art from the Heart along with crochet boy, who has now moved on to the magic of macramé.

The Hose Knows . . .

Your pantyhose define who you are. So here's a control-top guide to your personality.

For each of these questions, if you answered A, B, C, or D then you are the following:

A. Sexy Sheer
B. Crimson Thigh Highs
C. Navy Support
D. Barely There

A. Sexy Sheer—You have nothing to hide. You're a trend-setter, unafraid of change, and a team leader and problem solver at home and on the job.

B. Crimson Thigh Highs—You're a fire-brand in the office and at home. When trouble strikes, you throw a hissy fit and insult the PTA president or a nosy coworker who gets in your way.

C. Navy Support—You're the ultimate conservative; your career outlook is slow and steady. On the homefront, you do everything you can to make everyone happy but complain about it every step of the way.

D. Barely There—You're the mysterious
   coworker who is always reachable but
   never in the office. At home, you're still
   getting a mani/pedi while your child is
   waiting for to you pick him up from his
   weekly trapeze lesson. You may have
   your kids enrolled in dozens of activities, but you've never actually watched
   your child compete in a single game.

A Panty for Your Thoughts . . .

IF YOU are sexy sheer, congratulations—you
are a Role Mommy through and through. Keep
those work/life priorities in order, continue
to speak your mind, and do what you love
and no one will ever snag you, no matter how
hard they try to bring you down.

If you're unhappy with your current career
situation or if the kids are stressing you out
at home, that crimson outlook will eventually
land you in hot water unless you decide to
make a change.

Stop expecting everyone else to prop you
up, navy support girl—make a decision and
start doing the things you've always wanted to

do. When you're at home, don't let your kids or carpool mates walk all over you—if you become the ultimate pushover then you will only have yourself to blame.

If you're barely there, make sure you still get your work turned in on time even when you've slipped away for a massage appointment. A word of caution—the mom who is barely there at home gives all of us a bad name. Think twice before you dash off in another direction when your kids want to spend quality time with you. They're only young once so enjoy it now, because before you know it, they'll hit high school and will be avoiding you like the plague.

Role Mommy
Reality Check

Although you may think it's impossible, if you give yourself a sexy sheer makeover you may find that you'll be able pull it together at home and in the office without a snag or a run. No one ever said that managing your career along with your family would be easy. But it's never too late to realign your seams.

OUR LIVES...
B.C. before children
and
after diapers A.D.

Blackberry

B.C. The delicious tart fruit you'd pick as you meander down a secluded dirt path while vacationing in the mountains.

BlackBerry™

A.D. The addictive electronic device that enables you to return to that favorite vacation spot with your kids and still be plugged into civilization as you respond to a litany of emails sent by your boss, coworkers, spammers, friends, and potential clients. There is one problem; it's difficult to pick a blackberry and send a message from one at the same time.

4

Sometimes, a Girl's Gotta Fake It

GET YOUR mind out of the gutter, that's not what we mean. Although after ten years of marriage and sleeping with the same man night after night, who are we to judge?

The bottom line is that in your personal life, just like your professional life, there's nothing wrong with a little strategic "faking it" every now and again.

Once upon a time it would have been virtually impossible to pass off your free time as financially productive. Well, cyber-up Cinderella, it's a whole new world out there. Although we're not condoning lying on your time card or padding your billable hours, we are saying that every now and then, it's okay for your boss to believe you're working from your home office when you're really in the fitting room at Filene's during their winter blowout sale. And, when your daughter has a ballet recital the very same day your annual report is due, don't worry, wi-fi can do wonders for you. Remember, there's no harm in a little creative telecommuting now and then.

God bless the BlackBerry. It's a working mother's lifesaver as well as lifeline. Does it really matter whether you're answering those emails from the office, shoe department, bowling alley, Starbucks, or Musical Munchkins class? We say no. But just like everything in life, there's a right way and a wrong way to do things. So here it is, just between us girls, our guide to faking it. Enjoy your lesson—just don't tell your boss or husband that we're the ones who steered you over to the dark side.

Make Nice with the Geeky I.T. Guy

THE SAME strange and sweaty man who drives you crazy when he sets up camp in your cubicle suddenly becomes your very best friend when you're out of the office and losing it when your laptop goes down. Yes, the guy who has you grabbing for the Lysol every time he approaches your desk suddenly takes on superhuman qualities when you leave the comfy confines of your office. Don't kid yourself. The forty-year-old with the *Star Trek* fixation who still lives with his mom is the great defender of your flexible work schedule and working-mom-friendly lifestyle. Without the resident Trekky Tech Geek, there's no way you could maneuver the technical abyss that allows you to telecommute. So smile, be charming and witty, engage in a little ridiculous small talk, and remember, it won't kill you every now and then to say, "Hey, did you hear George Takei on Howard Stern this morning? Who knew Sulu was gay?" Remember, a little kindness goes a long way and a little faking it will take you even further.

Keep Your Mouth Shut

THINK BACK to tenth grade when you French-kissed that football player under the bleachers and you swore your girlfriend Suzy

to secrecy. Remember how it felt the next day
when the entire class pointed at you and whis-
pered "tramp" as you walked down the hall?
We hope you learned your lesson, because
the office is nothing but a big old high school
with older, balder, and fatter kids. Nobody can
keep a secret. There's absolutely no reason
to tell your coworkers that you're heading
out to read *Where the Wild Things Are* to your
preschooler's class. Your office is full of "Wild
Things" who happen to be very jealous that
you've carved out a nice little schedule for
yourself. When you're working from home,
silence is more than golden, it's mandatory.

Get Rid of the Evidence

NOTHING PUTS up a red flag faster than
those fatal four little words, "sent by wireless
BlackBerry." Now's the perfect time to call
your new buddy Edwin in I.T. and ask him
how to get rid of the evidence. No one will
think twice when you respond to emails via
BlackBerry at, say, 7:30 a.m. or 7 p.m. But, do
you really want your boss to know you're not
in the office (again) at 3 p.m. when he's out of
town on a business trip, you're supposed to be

working on a presentation with Mindy from marketing, and she's expecting your contributions within the hour? The truth is that it's your turn to volunteer for Brownies, so you bring along your PDA and let your fingers do the talking. You'd be surprised how creative you can be on the fly. While the girls are constructing a log cabin made out of popsicle sticks, email some pearls of wisdom to your coworker, and in five seconds flat she'll be thanking you for your brilliant observations.

BlackBerry Meltdown

Beth's Story

ALTHOUGH A BlackBerry is a necessary appendage when working from home, I fully admit there is a downside to having an overly dependent relationship with a palm-sized lifesaver. During a recent business trip, my trusty handheld companion officially experienced a meltdown. I managed to abuse it so much over the preceding six months that the thing just went completely haywire. Of course, it malfunctioned during the worst possible time—I was coordinating a huge red-carpet event with several big-name celebrities and producers who kept firing off emails to me about their flights and hotels, but all I could do was frantically press buttons that were malfunctioning like R2D2 in the first *Star Wars* movie.

To be completely candid, at the time I felt like an addict suffering from withdrawal. That red light was flashing incessantly, almost mocking me to grab the BlackBerry and try to access my messages even though I knew it was on the fritz. I gave it a whirl anyway, and the thing started having a mind of its own—picking websites I didn't want to visit or attempting to send messages to people I didn't need to reach or want to contact at all.

I can't imagine what I could have done to break the damn thing. All I'd done was use it to access my work email plus three personal email accounts, find websites and directions, make the occasional phone call—heck, if it could dispense money, I'd be plugging in my ATM password, too.

My husband always gets annoyed with me when I'm trying to return a quick message while I'm out at dinner with him and the kids.

I never really understood what the issue was until I was kicked out of the BlackBerry clique. As I stared longingly at that red flashing light, I began to discover that legions of chronic emailers and texters are completely detached and distracted from the real world. I rely on technology to help me master both life and work, and I never thought that my BlackBerry use was detracting from my life, but you know what, it was.

I've been known to cross city streets while responding to an email, and once I narrowly escaped injury from a bike messenger who swerved to avoid knocking me over. While in my car, I've glanced over at the red light and been tempted to access my emails while waiting for green. I've even noticed the message waiting indicator in the middle of the night while I was charging my PDA and contemplated reaching for it at three in the morning just to see who was trying to get in touch with me.

But here's the cold-hearted truth—I am not a brain surgeon, or a lawyer, or an accountant, or even a police detective, for that matter. I am a publicist. Even though I'm always connected to my office and to a demanding cadre of agents, managers, producers, and actors who sometimes work my last nerve—especially when I'm coordinating a massive press trip for all of them to travel from Los Angeles to Chicago and they keep changing their minds about their flights—it's not life or death.

And in the end, when I was on my own I managed to get everyone what they needed, even without the help of my BlackBerry—imagine that.

Master the Art of Call Forwarding

THIS IS indeed an art form. What's really important here? Where you're sitting when you get that phone call or what you say when your mobile starts ringing an annoying tune? So what if that call originates in your office, gets routed to your kitchen, is forwarded again to your cell phone, and you fumble for it while sitting in a booth at Friendly's? Who cares as long as you get the damn call? You know the old rule of business and dating—when you're sitting by the phone, it never rings. So get up, get the kids from school, and take them for ice cream, and when the phone rings, tell them you'll pay them each a dollar to keep mum. They'll instantly become your accomplices. With your kids as coconspirators, you will become a guru of out-of-office answering.

Role Mommy
Reality Check

We've read the rule books written by generations before us and realized that they just don't work. It's time we set new standards, ones that set us apart from those time-clock-punching, rule-abiding 9-to-5-ers who came before us.

We say ditch that desk and say so long to those shackles. If you have drive, ambition, and an uncanny ability to multitask, you, too, can bring home the bacon, turn it into a soufflé, and create a diorama of the Mesozoic era, all before 8 p.m.

BlackBerry Rules to Live By

1. **No deal making while dining.** Never pull the BlackBerry out during dinner. You may land an important meeting, but your kids will probably instigate a full-on food fight while you're typing away. Not only will you need to duck from the tater tots being tossed across the room but you'll also be in the direct line of fire from the death stares your husband shoots in your direction.

2. **Don't D.U.I.B.** Seriously, don't even think about driving under the influence of your BlackBerry. Women already get a bad rap as drivers—don't give the guys any more ammo. We don't care how fast you are on that thing, it is simply unacceptable to steer with your knees while your fingers are typing away.

3. **Use your words.** Your BlackBerry is a valuable business tool, but don't rely on it for everything. Sometimes, nothing can or should replace a good old fashioned phone

call. Trust us, your mother would rather hear your voice than read "HOW R U?"

4. **BlackBerries need bedtimes, too.** Hide the BlackBerry in a drawer after 7 p.m. each night—the later you respond to emails, the more your boss will expect you to answer an urgent message at midnight.

5. **Play hard to get.** There's something to be said for being a little aloof sometimes. You don't have to answer each and every email the second you receive it, and you don't want everyone thinking that you sit around all day staring at that little screen (even if you do). If you find yourself responding to emails over the weekend, in the early morning hours, or late at night, then you are officially obsessed. Admitting you have a problem is always the first step.

OUR LIVES...
B.C. before children
and
after diapers A.D.

Tight Jeans

B.C. The acid-washed Levi 501s you poured yourself into before heading out for ladies night margarita madness with your girlfriends.

A.D. Any pair of pants you attempt to squeeze yourself into after gaining 50 pounds from your pregnancy. Your new motto: I Love Lycra.

5

Dress to De-stress

REPEAT AFTER us: It's OK to wear the same clothes for three days straight and even sleep in them, as long as you change your underwear.

You know you've done it. Come on, after gaining 50 pounds with each pregnancy and nursing till your boobs look like two deflated balloons, it's time to face facts. Those size twos with the hoochie mama hemlines lingering in the back of your closet will never see the light of day again. How dare Janet Jackson call what happened to her during the Super Bowl a wardrobe malfunction? Any working mother knows that a true wardrobe malfunction is trying to figure out what to wear when everything that still fits around your ever-expanding hips is covered in spit-up or spaghetti sauce or is so ridiculously out of style that some flamboyant fashionista would think you were retro if you wore it.

Ah, the wardrobe dilemma—the good, the bad, and the very, very painfully ugly.

Dressing for Flex

FOR THOSE who work from home or have flexible work schedules—life is indeed beautiful. There's no need to worry about what fits, what makes you look fat, and why muumuus will never be fashionable again. Who cares if your shoes scream last season when you're emailing orders from Gymboree or tallying up your sales tax from your kitchen table? Gone are the days of the sensible suit and freshly pressed pants—it's time to embrace the aroma of tumble dried T-shirts and sweats that take you straight from sleep to school to the soccer field and then home again to tackle those spread sheets. Remember, unless you've taken the idea of the flexible work schedule to the extreme and are running a phone sex business from your family room, no one is going to ask what you are wearing when you're getting down to business.

Now, when it's time to actually leave the comforts of your home office and venture out into the real world for errands, don't worry about being seen in the same ensemble over and over again. That's why God created big fluffy coats and curbside drop-off for kids: they can disguise a multitude of style sins. If you're wondering what Betty in the Beemer behind you would think if she knew you were on day three of your black yoga pants and green hoodie combo, don't worry. Betty hasn't bothered to wear a bra since she went wireless and moved her marketing company to her basement a month ago.

Dressing for the Desk

ALTHOUGH WE would like to think that you can actually build a multimillion dollar company in the comfort of your Keds, let's not kid ourselves. Even those of us with the most flexible of flextime arrangements do actually have to attend meetings and have some face-to-face interaction now and then. For those occasions, your lucky flannel pajamas won't cut it; no matter how comfy they are and how many deals you've managed to close in them. You're going to have to bite the bullet and get yourself a few grown-up outfits.

At this point in your life, if you can wrap your head around spending $400 on a Diane Von Furstenberg wrap dress and still make your preschool payments on time, good for you and happy full price retail rip-off shopping. But, if like most working moms, your taste tends more toward discount than designer these days, all you need are a few key pieces and a lot of attitude. Remember, you don't have to shop at Nieman Marcus (aka Needless Mark-up) to make it look like you're a billion-dollar business babe. Invest in a few key pieces—great neutral pants and a few fabulous tops, and you're good to go. Forget what the fashion magazines say, who cares if *Harper's Bazaar* declares chartreuse is the new black. Keep it simple, sister. Black is always back. Add a few strategic splashes of color, some amazing accessories, and no one will ever know that fabulous statement pin strategically placed over your left boob is hiding the spillover from Molly's morning oatmeal.

Now we know what you're thinking, who has time to hit the stores and actually go shopping? We know you really want to make it to Macy's, but let's face facts—it may take a while before you can get there. Today, we say Tar-jay all the way (that is, Target). You multitask in every other aspect of your life—so why not when it comes to shopping? You really do need to stock up on school supplies and laundry detergent, so why not get it all done at once? Here's a little secret—hit the candy aisle first, pick up a ring pop to keep the kids busy, and make a beeline for the Isaac Mizrahi display.

Who can find fault with a cute little $12.99 sparkly sweater thrown over your basic black pants? And at Target prices, we say pick up that cute sweater in every color. Everyone will be too busy staring at you in your adorable top to notice that you've worn the same pair of black pants for every meeting for the past six months, even if those pants have the stretched out elastic that's left over from your last pregnancy. Really, they'll never know.

Then, when that pampered princess from accounting asks where you got your oh-so-adorable top, lie through your teeth. It's all in the attitude. Tap into those smoke and mirror acting skills you fine-tuned when you managed to finance your company from your cell phone while getting a blowout, and your Target special will look and feel like it came right off the runway. Then, you can race home to get back into your sweats and fuzzy pink slippers just in time for your 5:30 p.m. conference call.

In Case of Job Interview: Break Glass

ALL RIGHT, ladies, it's time to call in reinforcements. There's no room for a fashion faux pas when you're just one interview away from your dream job. Picture it, a new gig with awesome benefits, flexible work hours, extravagant expense account, on-site daycare, and did we mention a salary that will finally stop you from having an aneurysm every time the AmEx bill shows up?

You know you're perfect for this job. You're qualified and confident. There's only one thing standing in your way—your wardrobe. You can't ace the interview wearing your Liz Lange for Target leftovers when the CEO you're meeting with is the best dressed woman on the planet. Forget the flip flops, Manolos are a must-have in this situation. Whoever said eyes are the windows to the soul had it totally wrong. Today's soul sister could care less about your eyes, she's checking out your shoes, your bag, and your belt, and don't think she didn't notice your coat as you casually placed it over the chair with the Roberto Cavalli label facing up for all to see.

In her best-selling book, Hillary Clinton said it best: "It takes a village." So, unless you want to saunter into that meeting looking like the village idiot, you'll phone a friend, or two, or three, and plan a shopping spree in your best-dressed friends' closets.

Then, when you ace the interview and your new boss pays you a compliment on how accomplished, pulled together, and elegant you are, you simply smile and say, "I settle for nothing but the best, both professionally and personally."

Now, once you land the job, it's best to ease back into your own wardrobe. You can't go cold turkey here and have your chic CEO thinking you're nothing but a big old fashion fraud. The trick here is to keep borrowing your friends' clothes and gradually start introducing your own things into the mix.

Then, by the time they start noticing the formula stains on your suits, they'll be so impressed with your creativity they won't care you're not a couture queen.

A Pregnant Pause

Yvette's Red Carpet Catastrophe

IF YOU'RE expecting, congratulations—all rules go out the window, even ours. When you are pregnant, you are allowed to wear whatever you want for as long as it fits you. It's tough enough worrying about pasteurized milk, processed meats, and contracting all those crazy diseases you read about in *What to Expect When You're Expecting*. You don't need to be worrying about looking cute when you feel like a cow. I gave up on cute and caved in to comfort after one particularly traumatic turn on the red carpet one night as I was covering an A-list fashion industry event.

At seven months pregnant, I was feeling like a bloated bovine but pulled it together in what I thought was a cute little top and jacket as I staked out my spot among the camera crews and paparazzi. In walked Sarah Jessica Parker, Molly Sims, and several other fabulous and fashionable stars—all graciously doing their interviews and congratulating me on my big belly. Then, a HUGE designer, we're talking fashion icon with a cultlike following, made his way up the red carpet and right up to my microphone. "So what's your number one style tip for women?" I asked. That's when it happened, the unthinkable, the ultimate style setback for any woman, let alone a pregnant one. This world famous designer looked me up and down, smiled, leaned in, grabbed hold of my top, and said "Button your jacket, you'll look thinner."

I tried to keep my cool, but as you can imagine, my prenatal hormones were raging. Are you for real? I was so shocked that I was actually speechless. I said nothing as he sauntered away from me. But that wasn't the case for my paparazzi partners in crime. The same motley crew who thought nothing of stomping over me and my pregnant belly to get a shot of Beyonce and Naomi Campbell during fashion week (yes, this actually happened, and I had to be rescued by security guards) went nuts.

"Hey, she's pregnant. What the hell's the matter with you?" they shouted.

Thanks, fashion fool. I guess it was the womanly curves that threw you off. Don't worry, stick to stick figures. We've got the real women covered on this end.

Role Mommy
Reality Check

Sure, we long for the days of our designer wardrobes. But come on, it's time to stop staring longingly at the little black dress you'll never fit into again and think of the greater good. Having children is no excuse to stop taking care of your body or stop taking pride in how you look, but it's time to lighten up and stop being so hard on yourself. Eventually the pounds will fall off and you'll fit back into some of your clothes. As for those skinny jeans that no longer make it past your kneecaps—get rid of them. Clean out that closet and give those old clothes to charity. It's time to get over it. Your waist may be fuller, but so is your life.

TIME-OUT

Seven Reasons Why I Can't Fit into Seven Jeans

1. I'm still trying to lose the same 20 pounds I gained from the birth of my son, who is now four years old.
2. It gives me painful flashbacks to when I was a chubby twelve-year-old who couldn't squeeze into her Sergio Valente's.
3. Those vanity sizes only fit mannequins, waif models, Paris Hilton, and those Olsen twins.
4. I'd rather spend $140 relaxing with a glass of wine at a romantic dinner for two.
5. I'm waiting for Ten jeans to make a comeback.
6. If I do actually squeeze into the jeans, I'll have to run straight to the emergency room because it will cut off the circulation in my thighs.
7. Seven is not a lucky number when you're trying to yank it over your protruding posterior.

OUR LIVES...
B.C. before children
and
after diapers A.D.

Morning Ritual

B.C. After a solid 8–10 hours of sleep, the alarm would wake you at 7 a.m. You'd pour a pot of freshly brewed coffee, hit the treadmill then catch the morning news. Sometimes, you'd add a quickie to your morning repertoire; in this case, you'd leave for work with a big smile on your face, ready to face the day.

A.D. After ushering your three-year-old to the potty at 12:30 a.m. and the monsters out of your five-year-old's closet at 3 a.m., you end up with about 4 hours of choppy sleep at best before the alarm wakes you at 6 a.m. As you sleepily slap together PB&J sandwiches for lunch, a big smile crosses your face when you realize the class guinea pig you've hosted for the past week is finally going back to school today and taking her smelly cage with her.

6

Everything I Learned about Parenthood I Picked Up on My Commuter Train

Beth's Story

SOME SWEAR by Oprah. Others peruse *Parenting*. For crafty types there's *Good Housekeeping* or Martha Stewart. And for those who rely on the experts, it's a self-help book all the way. As a busy working mom with barely any time to watch TV or read, a family fix by Doctor Phil is out of the question. So,

I do the next best thing, I ride the railroad. I get all my tried and true parental and career advice while aboard the 8:49 a.m. commuter train. If it weren't for Robin, Erica, Mei Mei, and sometimes Susan, who makes our train if she's running incredibly late, I'd probably be reduced to relying on *Supernanny* or late night reruns of *Roseanne* for hands-on how-to advice.

Who needs Dr. Spock when I have the Metro North Railroad? Our thirty-three-minute gab session is chock full of amazing information. In between sips of coffee, we bring each other up to date on the best pediatricians, the latest birthday party themes, summer camps, home renovations, local real estate finds, and great kid friendly restaurants. We even manage a little networking of our own, followed up by a quick consult on what to do with a seven-year-old who still prefers to sleep in your bed. Our morning coffee klatch is something I look forward to every workday because my commuter girlfriends have provided me with some of the best advice a mom could ask for.

Before you start saying you don't commute to work and you spend most of your time stuck in your home office or carpooling the kids to Cub Scouts, there are plenty of other places to uncover great advice for the home, work, and everything in between. So, if you're primed for some new parenting advice that you won't find on TV or in the pages of a Dr. Sears best-seller, here are some unorthodox alternatives.

The Nail Salon

THE SALON is a perfect place to eavesdrop on conversations by total strangers. The key here is to keep it local; always pick a nail place in your own town to get the most out of your salon secret mission. Just close your eyes and pretend you're really enjoying that cuticle massage as you listen in on the two women getting French manicures across from you. Take mental notes as they discuss which teachers their kids love, give too much homework, or are more than ready for early retirement.

As you're sitting under the dryer, they're sure to dive into a little local gossip. Since you've been MIA at almost every PTA event this year, this is the best chance you'll have at finding out which neighborhood kids are on the honor roll and for which ones "away at camp" really means another stint in the juvenile delinquent facility.

If you stick to places strategically located near your children's school, you're sure to learn everything you need to know about academic and extracurricular activities. Your fact-finding mission will be most successful if you time it for midday when the kids are still in school and the moms meet for their pedicures. Now we know you're usually not around during the day because you're busy working—but never underestimate the nail salon. Knowledge is power, and the useful parenting nuggets you can pick up at Nails Today may be worth burning a vacation day. Besides, you know you're in desperate need of a wax anyway.

Whole Foods, Trader Joes, Ralph's, and Other Trendy Supermarkets

WE CAN'T tell you how many times we've bumped into friends while racing down the aisles of our favorite supermarket. Our worlds literally collided when Yvette and Beth bumped into each other in the produce section of Stew Leonard's one errand-filled Saturday morning. Beth's cart was loaded to the brim with fruit snacks and pre-packaged meals while Yvette's was spilling over with organic produce and the makings of that evening's culinary masterpiece.

In the five minutes we rolled down the aisles together, Beth got a lesson on how pre-made pie crust can change your life and Yvette got the scoop on the brand new chicken nuggets Beth had discovered in the frozen food section. So grab a cart, lose that list, and listen in on the chatfest in aisle four. Those girl-friends who just met up in the frozen veggie section may unlock the secrets to getting your kids to finally eat their spinach.

Any Coffee House in Any Mall in America

THERE THEY are, the coffee klatch. You can't miss them as they hold court in the food court. That's them in the large round corner table surrounded by soy lattes and their latest purchases. These fashion plates are the perfect moms to get your fashion fix from.

Grab yourself an iced cappuccino and a ringside seat. If you haven't had time to read *Vogue* in months, not to worry—these ladies are your crash course in what's current. With just one glance, they can tell you if bobs are back, if animal prints are in, and if this season is all about ghetto chic or glam.

To these moms, shopping is a sport, and we can bet they're competing to see whose baby tops the best-dressed list. Chances are their kids are nowhere in sight during your reconnaissance mission. Too distracting— fashionistas need to focus while they're shopping. Don't be discouraged—to find out what's trendy for today's tykes, just follow the trail of evidence and steal a glance at their packages. If everyone is lugging those precious pink Lilly Pulitzer bags, then sweet florals and dresses are the way to go. If they're carting around Children's Place or Limited Too gear, then bling is in.

Now, by the time they're ready for a second round of lattes, lean in. They're sure to start spilling the beans. Even the best-dressed mom can't resist a bargain. These women hold the key—the secret locations of the ultimate fashion do: the sample sale. Try not to be too obvious with your eavesdropping here, they hold this information sacred and don't like sharing it with just anyone. But, if you're smart and strategic, you may just uncover the legendary location of that which all mothers dream about but only dare speak about in hushed tones, the holy grail of haberdashery . . . the GapKids outlet.

The Office

THERE'S NO better place than the office for a quick lesson on navigating the working mother minefield. Forget what your mother taught you, here eavesdropping is not rude, it's a requirement. There's nothing wrong with a little listening in now and then for a quick reality check on how your cubicle mate is juggling her chaotic life. Overhear as Always Available Alice volunteers for yet another ten-day trip to Detroit, and then calls her staff of nannies to work out their schedules while she's away. Finally, she phones home to tell her son that Juanita, the cleaning lady, will be lending a hand and filling in at parent's night. Then she hits speed dial and demands to speak to her family therapist, trying to figure out why her ten-year-old is still wetting the bed.

Walk slowly as you round the corner by Guilty Gilda's desk. Once again, she's obsessively watching her nanny cam and making origami turkeys for the preschool Thanksgiving feast. She puts the scissors down and stops pasting turkey beaks on the birds only as her boss stops by to tell her that she was passed up for the latest promotion. She wonders why, as she walks to the copy machine to make five hundred pilgrim party invites for the elementary school assembly and races out the door at 3:15 to make it to the party store before they run out of Native American napkins.

Role Mommy
Reality Check

Forget reality television and those serious how-to hardcover books: For time-strapped moms who are always on the go, real life is the best and most educational way to uncover priceless parenting tips. It's all around you, endlessly informative, funnier than anything we've seen on television, and best of all, it's free.

OUR LIVES...
B.C. **before children**
and
after diapers A.D.

Road Trip

B.C. You and your college girl-friends blasting cheesy 1980s music while on a twenty-four-hour drive to Daytona.

A.D. A minivan piled high with kid paraphernalia—strollers, car seats, luggage, fruit snacks, and two kids fighting in the back seat constantly asking you to fix the DVD player while torturing you with the same bloody question: ARE WE THERE YET???

7

Me, Myself, and My Minivan

Mommy Mobile Quiz

1. My first car was a
   A. Trendy sports car with a moon roof and tinted windows.
   B. Volkswagen Beetle, Golf, or Cabriolet.
   C. Mom or Dad's hand-me-down midsize sedan.
   D. A used Dodge Dart that I bought from a college burnout.

2.   My current car is a
   A. Honda Odyssey, Mazda MPV, Toyota
      Sienna, Dodge Caravan, or other boxy
      minivan.
   B. Ford Explorer, Toyota Land Cruiser,
      Acura MDX, or another SUV
   C. A two-seater sports car minus the
      passenger airbag so my child can sit in
      the front.
   D. A Volvo station wagon, SUV, or sedan.
      I'm obsessed with safety so it's Volvo all
      the way.

For some of us, it was the sleek little sports
car. For others, it was a yellow cab and the
promise of a designated driver always on
hand after a night of cocktailing.

Our relationships with cars have changed
considerably since our precious little passengers
came into our lives and we became obsessed
with car seats, tethers, and the ins and outs of
the latch system. Now, instead of candy red
convertibles, we drive mommy mobiles—
station wagons, SUVs, and yes, even the minivan.
Remember, looks can be very deceiving—
sometimes, you are not what you drive.

From MX3 to MPV

Beth behind the Wheel

"EXCUSE ME ma'am, which car is yours?" asks a parking lot attendant who has just handed off the keys of a silver Mercedes convertible to a 40-year-old nattily dressed businessman.

"It's the dark blue MPV," I respond confidently, with eyes gazing off in the direction of someone else's orient blue BMW 5 series.

"An MPV? That's the minivan right?" Oops, there it is. In an instant, my cover is blown. I may be dressed the part of high-powered executive, but the moment my chariot arrives, I am no match for the power players around me. I am mommy, watch me drive.

From the self-assured glare to the embarrassing stare, long gone are the days when the parking attendant would nod approvingly while handing over the keys to my candy apple red Mazda MX3.

Many chart success by the vehicles they drive, but in my life, my choice of cars has run in direct opposition with the direction of my career. In 1991, my journey began as I pursued a master's degree in journalism at

NYU while working parttime as a junior publicist at a public relations agency whose clients included *Geraldo, The Joan Rivers Show*, and *A Current Affair*. During those early days, when all I did was answer phones and fax press releases, I had my first brush with fame, riding the elevators with the legendary journalistic chain gang from *60 Minutes*, and passing Joan Rivers' dog Spike—who has since passed on—who piddled through the halls while I delivered press clippings.

Despite the excitement of my first real job, what I remember most from that time of my life is my car. With my measly paycheck, I managed to scrape together enough money each month to lease a Mazda MX3, an expensive looking yet affordable sports car that would put a smile on anyone's face as I passed them by on the road. I still wax nostalgic recalling the times I'd be waiting for a traffic light on the West Side Highway while catching friendly glances from several pedestrians who would give me a thumbs-up and mouth the words nice car. Little did they know I was still sleeping in my parent's house in a converted basement apartment. During the year that

I drove my MX3 from Brooklyn to midtown Manhattan, I was wide-eyed, hungry for success, and ready to conquer the world.

Fifteen years later, I've managed to carve out a nice place for myself in the TV industry. Over the years, I have ridden in limos with the likes of Tom Selleck, William Petersen, Ray Romano, Simon Cowell, Mark Harmon, Doris Roberts, Marg Helgenberger, Danny Aiello, Patricia Heaton, Kevin James, and many others whose limo rides lasted longer than their stints on television.

On the home front, I moved from Brooklyn to Central Park West. I left my dad with my MX3, met my future husband, moved with him to Queens, got married, and bought a house in the burbs. Then I got pregnant and bought an SUV.

Some Ugly Vehicle—an SUV is a mother's first rite of passage into the world of parenthood. Convinced we were way too hip for a minivan, we leased a bright green Subaru Forester for three years and traversed the highways, back roads, and jug handles of the tri-state area with our daughter gleefully enjoying the ride behind us in her comfy car seat. When we became pregnant a second time, however, we couldn't resist temptation. Calling was a minivan with a third row, plus more room for our junk—resist, resist, resist . . . acquiesce. So, from an MX3 to now, our family cruises throughout Westchester, Connecticut, the Hamptons, and Manhattan in a fully loaded, dark blue, gulp, Mazda MPV—aka a minivan.

Sure it has a DVD player, leather interior, and electronic doors, but that's where the luxury package ends. Those convenient doors don't work during inclement weather and the supple leather chairs are covered by two booster seats that hide a mountain full of crumbs, toys, and debris—artifacts from road trips taken long ago.

The amount of junk in our minivan could rival a garbage barge. On a typical afternoon you can find cookie crumbs, lollipop wrappers, stuffed animals, shoes, deflated balloons, dated birthday invitations, scotch tape for presents wrapped on the fly, flat fountain soda, gas station receipts, Mapquest directions to places we visited months ago, and sticky substances that would otherwise cause a bug infestation if our minivan wasn't made of indestructible steel.

I recently heard a story about a parent who left the sunroof open in his minivan and two uninvited guests hopped in and went to town. When the husband was sent out to the store to buy milk, he was ambushed by two raccoons that were having a field day inside his food-infested garbage truck on wheels.

Let's face it. Our vans may not be white, but they may as well read SANITATION in big black letters across one of our electronic sliding doors.

While my husband drives his sporty BMW to his office, I am the proud driver of our MPV. Dressed in my favorite Ann Taylor Loft suit, I place my iced coffee in the cup holder, plug in my iPod adapter, flip on the songs I used to sing to in the '80s and '90s (Who doesn't love a little Annie Lennox in the morning?), and head to Manhattan to my favorite parking garage, the same one I've been frequenting since my MX3 days. But here's the big difference. Today, when I arrive in Manhattan, no one stares and smiles at my *Chico & the Man* van. Most give me dirty looks if I'm in the crosswalk, or they just keep moving without giving my wheels a second glance.

While creeping along to the parking garage, bottles rolling up and down the aisles, I fling a toy that has rolled under the brake pedal to the back row and at that moment I think to myself, what has become of my driving life? I am so not cool anymore.

I own a minivan.

What's next? Will I start plastering the back of my car with nerdy bumper stickers like "My Kid Is an Honor Student" and "Proud to Be a Soccer Mom"?

What kind of twisted sitcom did I wind up in where I drop off a car shaped like a big box at a parking lot, cab it to the Four Seasons to pick up an A-list celebrity and her entourage, whisk her away for a day of press appearances in a stretch limousine, bid adieu when the job is done, and return to that box on wheels so I can come back home to whip up a dinner that actually tastes good, take the kids to the ice cream truck, and get them into their pajamas with teeth brushed . . . all before 9 p.m.?

There's something about a minivan that robs you of your identity. Twenty years ago, we had the world at our feet and were infatuated with the latest sports cars—I had friends with RX7s, 280ZXs, and Toyota Celicas. Today, they drive Honda Odysseys, Town & Countrys, and Ford Explorers.

As they say, there's a thin line between love and hate and that's exactly where I am with my MPV. I guess it's because I secretly miss the days that people stared at my cool little car. Nobody stares anymore, unless they're the disapproving ones—how filthy can you keep a car anyway? Manny at the parking garage must think I'm an absolute mess. Even more embarrassing to admit, when we're at my parents' house and we go out for dinner without the kids, my husband and I ask to borrow their Volvo so the valet won't wince when we hand over the keys.

Even though I ride from time to time in limousines, these days I'm best known as mommy, the family's personal chauffeur. Though it hasn't been easy, I've come to accept that my minivan is my life—at least, my life right now. It's chaotic, and when the two boisterous passengers are on board, it's filled with voices rattling off a fusillade of questions, demands, and funny one-liners.

Role Mommy
Reality Check

I may sometimes long for the days when I tooled around in my sports car, but I'd never sell my mommy mobile short. I may have lost my cool when I gave up that cool car, but when I see the mischievous faces of my kids through my rearview mirror, I realize I gained much more in return.

TIME-OUT
Road Trip Games

When We Were Kids

- The Fifty State license plate game
- Punch buggy green, punch buggy red
- Staring contests
- Stop pinching me
- Read books
- Sing songs
- Make conversation
- Look out the window
- Sleep

TIME-OUT
Road Trip Games

With Our Kids

- Time how long it takes before your kids say "Are we there yet?"
- Silent contest—winner gets a fruit roll-up.
- Pick out the car Mommy should buy next.
- Play "Whose car is dirtier? Ours, or that lady in the Dodge Caravan?"
- Point out roadkill and identify the animal.
- Warn Mommy and Daddy when the cops are approaching.
- DVD Triple Feature—Shrek, Monster's Inc., and Finding Nemo. If you don't own a DVD player, play "Guess what movie they're watching in the car in front of us?"
- Play a round of "How long can you hold it in?" Winner gets to go to McDonalds. Loser gets to go, too.

OUR LIVES...

B.C. before children
and
after diapers A.D.

Dirty Laundry

B.C. The embarrassing piece of news your so-called best friend shared with your boyfriend after she caught you in a lip lock with the cutie you shared a Bunsen burner with in chemistry class.

A.D. Mismatched smelly socks, five pink onesies covered in dried spit-up, your husband's Fruit of the Looms, and any other articles of clothing that have been living in your hamper or hanging around at the bottom of your closet for the past week and a half.

8

Potty Mouth Training

POTTY MOUTH Training—The process by which a foul-mouthed, four-letter-word loving woman finally realizes that her potty mouth is like the embarrassing hairstyle that haunts her every time she opens her yearbook . . . sadly outdated, slightly toxic, and an environmental hazard. She decides to clean up her potty mouth and learn to speak the universal language of mommy. For some, the transition is effortless (we don't know any of these women). For others, it's a much more slow and painful process as they lose words like shit and damn from their vocabulary and replace them with more child friendly versions—poop and darn.

There's no doubt about it, as mothers, we're obsessed with potty training. We buy videos, DVDs, and books, spend a small fortune on pull-ups and portable potties, and, if we've really gone over the edge, even break into a song and dance routine when our toddlers manage a poopy in the potty. (Admit it—you know you did it at least once or twice.)

As fascinated as we are by the traditional type of potty training, there's another kind that's forgotten about, never written about, and quite simply, never even acknowledged. Frankly, we feel it's much more challenging than teaching your child to make a doo doo in the talking potty you spent $29.99 on. As parents, we're the ones who need a little help in this area. By the time we need to be potty mouth trained, we're sleep-deprived, over-whelmed, overworked, and exhausted. Learn a new language, yeah, add it to my to-do list. But trust us on this one, it's a to-do that must be done.

If you're new to the mommy game, you probably think you have some time before your little angel starts picking up her mommy's devilish dialogue and you need to start cleaning up your act (as well as ten diapers a day). Guess again. Get on the potty mouth program before it's too late. Just because that beautiful little baby of yours can't speak yet doesn't mean she's not hearing every single curse that comes streaming out of your mouth. And, trust us, she's saving up to spit it back out just when it will embarrass you the most.

It happened to our friend Endria. Picture the scene. Endria, a real estate broker, driving through traffic with her client beside her in the front seat and her two-year-old, Christina, strapped in the back. The women are chatting about business, the baby is playing with her toys, and suddenly, a car cuts them off.

Beep beep—Endria honks her horn.

"Asshole," chimes in Christina from the back seat.

Since infancy, Christina must have witnessed that same scenario dozens of times but never repeated it. No, why waste this zinger on family or friends? Let's wait until mommy is doing business in the car to bust out with this wonderful new word.

Mary Poppins for the New Millennium

"JUST A spoonful of sugar makes the expletives go down."

The sugar substitute. By far, the most important aspect of potty mouth training is the use of the sugar substitute. We're not talking Splenda or Sweet'N Low here, although we're sure you use those, too. No, we're talking about your filthy little four-letter word fixation. Maybe it's a work thing; we know how adrenaline-charged offices like newsrooms breed bad language. "She missed her deadline, shit!" "What do you mean your piece is 15 seconds over, damn it!" But once you become a mom, you quickly realize that there is nothing cute about a four-year-old saying the F word.

Remember when you dropped the F bomb after spilling coffee on your freshly pressed white blouse, just as you were running out the door, late again, for a big meeting? Well, that little scenario left more than just a stain. Jimmy was listening, and now he thinks it's show and tell time with his new word.

And so you succumb to using the sugar substitute. That is, substituting "sugar" or some other child friendly word for your favorite little naughty nuggets.

You take your children out for a day of errands and some idiot in an Audi cuts you off on the highway. You no longer yell, "ass," you simply shout "sugar."

The pimply faced kid at the fast food restaurant forgets your fries? You quickly ban "damn" from your vocabulary and dole out a healthy heaping of "darn it."

Just like the other pre-packaged placebos, these sugar substitutes do come with a warning. Be very careful when and how you use them. Although we don't necessarily condone cursing at home, we accept that sometimes at the office nothing does the trick like a tried and true blue streak. Just think how your staff would respond to you admonishing them by saying, "You came in $10,000 over budget? That's stinky." Some new hire with a big chip on his shoulder takes credit for your idea and you stand up and confront him in a meeting yelling, "You're full of poop!" Nope, that simply won't do. In that case, you can bet your ASS we won't be reaching for the sugar substitute.

Censor Thyself: When Your Kids Think They're Gossip Columnists

AS A publicist and television producer, we're in the business of making celebrities look good. It's not in our best interest to slam a star because, in the end, negative press will inevitably bite you in the ass—oops, we mean tushy. Although we do have plenty of tales to tell about some nasty personal publicist or demanding actress whose requests exceeded the national budget of Mozambique, we keep those juicy tidbits to ourselves and never utter a word to gossip columnists, who are always on the prowl for a mean-spirited exclusive that is sure to embarrass their celebrity prey.

But at the end of the day, when we head home, somehow that permanent zipper on our lips bursts open and we start spewing our true feelings with those around us, bashing friends, colleagues, and PTA moms in our wake.

Even though you may want to let loose, beware of what you say. Our kids may not work for Page Six, but they might as well be on the payroll. And as the saying goes, loose lips sink ships.

Want to chat about how chunky your neighbor's been looking lately? Wait until the kids are in bed. Can't wait to dish about the messy divorce going on down the street? If the kids are around, don't even think about it. And if you're planning on replacing your babysitter, by all means don't mention it to Junior—he's sure to tell Nanny and she's sure to call in sick at 6 a.m. And, whatever you do, do not, we repeat, do not bitch and moan about other kids in front of your children.

Case in point: Your child tells you that her friend's older brother smacked her in the head during a playdate while her little playmate just stood there pointing and laughing.

Your blood will be boiling at this point, steam coming out of your ears, and your maternal instinct to kill those little bastards will be taking over.

Stop.

Think before you respond.

Don't start going on a tirade about what devious monsters those children are because, if you do, rest assured that while you're in the office, your own little Liz Smith will share your commentary with her friend's mom the very next day. Trust us, this really happened to one of us, and as a result, we can't even walk into a room without getting icy stares from that mother who sometimes whispers and points in our direction whenever she thinks we're not looking. Newsflash! We see you. We're just too embarrassed to say we're sorry if we offended you and your two little demons.

When we decided to write this book, we promised to be honest. We swore to tell it like it is and not sugarcoat our experiences as working mothers—except for the sugar substitute, of course. We have a confession to make. As much as we truly believe in the need to potty mouth train, there are times that we do actually, intentionally, use bad language in front of our kids. Yes, Yvette is the guilty one here. But we can assure you, her unconventional methods are motivated by a higher cause.

It's All Greek to Me . . . Cursing for a Cause

Yvette's Confession

I AM guilty of teaching my children bad language. For our family, bad words aren't always reasons to give time-outs; sometimes, they're teaching tools.

I grew up bilingual, a first generation American in a Greek household. I want my children to grow up bilingual, to understand their Greek heritage and culture. We speak Greek at home and Christiana and Nicholas understand everything—getting them to speak Greek, that's another story.

I did everything humanly possible. We would sing songs, tell stories, and read books, whatever I could do to expose them to the language. They loved every minute of it, but at the end of the day, I would ask them a question in Greek and they would respond in English. It drove me crazy.

So, when everything else seemed to fail, I did the unthinkable. I thought of the one thing that would make my children speak the language of the Gods, some good old gutter talk.

It hit me one day in the grocery store, when the produce wasn't up to par. I leaned over and said, "Christiana, those cherries look like skata (shit)."

Christiana looked at me like I was nuts. (Gasp) "Mommy, that's a bad word."

"I know, Koukla (doll), but I said it in Greek so nobody here knows what we're talking about. Isn't it great to have our own private language that we can tell secrets in?"

That's all it took.

Give a four-year-old a secret and she's yours forever. Now, both of my children will switch effortlessly back and forth from Greek to English. When I want them to speak Greek, I slip in something slightly naughty and they're mine.

Family Potty Mouth Training

NOW, JUST when you think you have your potty mouth training under control comes yet another complication, the family. That's right, as if we didn't have enough to worry about already, we soon find the rest of the family needs to be potty mouth trained as well. And as Beth found out, sometimes they're the toughest ones to tackle.

Grandpa Fixit's Foul Mouth

Beth's Dad Does It Again

MY FATHER is a prime example of an adult who is oblivious to the fact that his two impressionable grandchildren are always in earshot when he yells out profanities after stubbing his big toe on the coffee table. Or when someone cuts him off in traffic, he yells "son of a bitch," not realizing that the two parrots in the back seat have just learned a new phrase. In high-pitched voices they squeal in delight, "Son of a bitch, son of a bitch!"

You see, it's quite hard for a sixty-five-year-old man to watch what he says in front of our children—he's been uttering these phrases since I was a child. In fact, some of my most memorable moments with my dad happened back in the 1970s when he tried to make our Plymouth Grand Fury start by swatting the steering wheel and shouting "Son of a bitch!" After the car started with those magical words, I was convinced that all it took was a curse to start cars, dishwashers, lawn mowers, and washing machines—if an appliance was on the fritz, just yell out "shit" and it started up again.

So Grandpa Fixit, as we like to call him, has now had a crash course in potty mouth training. Every time he utters the "S" word, he gets admonished by his granddaughter, who advises that he better watch what he says or else Grandma will give him a time-out.

Ewwww . . . How Insults Can Do More Damage Than Four-Letter Words

Beth's Story

I NEVER realized how the word "ewwww" could be completely insulting and embarrassing until my seven-year-old used it on two different occasions while commenting on the unsightly physique of two unsuspecting adults. The first was a good friend of ours who had packed on a few extra pounds over the years and thought nothing of walking around a vacation house we shared with him without his shirt on. Unfortunately, this fashion choice left him in the direct line of fire of my daughter, who stared at his oversized belly and exclaimed "EWWWWWWW!!!!" Lucky for us, he made light of the situation.

Unlucky for us was the day we forgot to tell our daughter not to use that word when the windows of our minivan were wide open and our neighbor was doing some shirtless tree pruning. Out of nowhere, we heard the infamous insult fly out of her mouth, "EWWWWW!!!" and when we looked over at our neighbor whose back hair was standing on end while he stared angrily in our direction, we rolled up the windows and tore out of sight. Actually, we parked the car, sent our daughter to her room, and then instructed her to write fifty times that she won't insult another person ever again.

Role Mommy Reality Check

There's much more to potty mouth training then just minding those four-letter words. When we're at work, we can't censor what our children are hearing from that nasty little kid swinging from the monkey bars or from the soap opera that our baby-sitter left on while she was making lunch. What we can do is instruct our kids that swearing and name calling can be hurtful. Just ask Beth, who still has painful flashbacks to being labeled Stubby Beth in the fourth grade. We all know that cursing may be an inevitable right of passage for our children, but insults should always be left at the curb.

POTTY MOUTH 101

Curse Word	Kiddy Version
Ass	Tush
Shit	Poop
Damn	Darn
Hell	Heck
F***	Fudge
Son of a bitch	Sugar
Asshole	Butthead
Moron	Silly guy
Idiot	Silly guy
Schmuck	Schmegeggie

Potty Mouth Odometer:
A Guide to Cursing in Your Car

Damn	You miss your exit on the highway.
A**	Someone cuts you off in traffic.
Putz	The same guy who cut you off gets pulled over by the cops.
Crap	You roll through a stop sign and get pulled over by the same cop who pulled over the putz.
S**t	A Happy Meal toy rolls under your brake pedal.
Son of a Bitch	You're on a conference call while driving (using a headset of course) and the coffee cover you thought was placed on your drink, pops off and saturates the outfit that just came back from the cleaners.
F***	You accidentally drop the contents of a chocolate milk container into your $300 designer bag.

OUR LIVES...
B.C. before children
and
after diapers A.D.

Party Animal

B.C. You, during happy hour, as you downed Jell-O shots, flirted with inappropriate man, and danced on tabletops.

A.D. The mangy rodent for which you paid an obscene amount of money to entertain the troops at your child's birthday party. But all that overpriced hairball does is make the kids cry and pee on your living room rug.

9

If You Can't Be with the One You Love, Playdate with the One You're With . . .

L ET'S FACE it. The life of a modern mom would not be complete without the playdate.

While at work, we get a voicemail from Playdate Penny who would love to pencil our child in for an afternoon of organized extra-curricular activities and we "accidentally" forget to call her back for days. Then there

are the times when the baby-sitter calls in
sick and we're desperate to find the Post-it
where we jotted down Playdate Penny's
phone number.

For some moms, scheduling playdates has
become a full-time job. They have it down to
a science, organizing and planning everything
from the kids to the carpool to the heart-
shaped sandwiches they'll serve as snack. We
applaud these women. They do an amazing
job and are the queens of playdates. Now, for
working mothers, it's a different story. We
already have full-time jobs and are stretched
so thin that we usually don't have the time,
energy, or sanity required to plan the perfect
playdate. Let's call those two-hour chunks of
socialized, structured play what they really
are—all work no play dates.

But the truth is, as much as we try to avoid
it, the playdate is here to stay. For those of
you new to the game, here's a simple guide to
help you survive the pitfalls of playdating, the
ones we loathe and the ones we love.

Because if you can't be with the one you
love, playdate with the one you're with.

Playdates We Loathe

Playdate Desperado. A lonely mother who is new to the neighborhood will stalk you and your child until you agree to come over to play for an afternoon. The truth is, she's the one desperate for a playdate and is using her child as bait. Out of pity or exhaustion, you finally give in and accept the offer, only to find you have nothing in common with this woman. To add insult to injury, the kids get into a major brawl, and before you can grab the doorknob to make your getaway, she's asking you for a second date and you desperately search your library of excuses to think of a believable reason as to why you can never return. Incidentally, contagious skin rashes work like a charm.

Playdate Cliques. On the rare occasion you do drop your child off at school, you see them gathering in the parking lot. Sporting trendy workout clothes, hair tied back in ponytails, light makeup application, the keys to their Lexus SUVs in one manicured hand and their pig-tailed child's hand in the other. Meet the playdate clique, or the "witches of preschool" as we like to call them, comprising women who do everything together, be it coffee, tennis, gym, and of course, playdates. If you happen to take a day off from work and have a run-in with the witches, they'll be sure to pretend not to know who you are and will intentionally box you out of their conversation. When you overhear them chat about their plans to take their little princesses to an afternoon origami workshop, don't feel bad that you're not on the invite list. Smile to yourself because you know that tomorrow, while they're chasing their kids at Chuck. E. Cheese's, you'll be back at work lunching and laughing with one of your favorite clients—who happens to be a working mom just like you.

Peculiar Playdates. Your kids get along great and your child begs, pleads, and moans to have a playdate with her newest friend. Only one problem, you find the parents kind of weird. It's like visiting the Addams Family. They were always friendly, but something was always just a little off-center. It's not like they've got Cousin It or that creepy hand named Thing bunking with them, but the mom is sporting that 1970s long-haired Morticia look, and the place seems to have a spooky Halloween feel to it and it's only March. The peculiar play-daters phone constantly, and if you still don't have caller ID, run, don't walk, to the nearest Radio Shack, or else you're doomed.

Playdate Piranhas. Jimmy seemed nice enough, but after inspecting the bite marks on your son's left arm, you realize it might be best to keep your child away from Hannibal Lecter-in-training. Biters, punchers, sword fighters, and swashbucklers can be scary when your child—a rule-abiding, Raffi-loving moppet—enters their world. Suddenly, your peaceful pixie starts picking up those bad habits, and the next thing you know, he's biting the dog. Rule of thumb for biters: if they break the skin during a playdate, they can't come back until they break the habit—if that doesn't happen until middle school, then sorry, but it's been nice knowing you.

Playdate Paranoia. This is the most stressful playdate by far. The mother brings her child to your house with a laundry list of things the kid can't eat, wear, smell, swallow, or touch. "Are you kosher? Are those crayons nontoxic, and do you use pesticides on your lawn? Is that coloring book age appropriate? We don't believe in television, and video games are out of the question. What about the beverages? If you don't have 2 percent growth hormone free organic milk then he'll just have water, not bottled, fluorinated tap water that's been filtered, of course."

You smile politely and make note of the checklist. But what you're really thinking is—Are you kidding me, lady? Are you intentionally raising your boy like John Travolta in that plastic bubble movie, and do you really want to allow him to have any interaction with my kid, whose favorite pastime is proudly proclaiming the booger he just picked is especially for you?

Playdates We Love

Playdate with a Pal. This is by far the best kind of playdate. In this scenario, you are taking your child to see one of his or her closest friends and mom just happens to be one of your friends, too. These are simple, enjoyable, and as close to heaven as humanly possible.

This always happens after work. You bring your kids over in their pajamas and they proceed to try on about 40 different costumes. Arguments are kept to a minimum, your wine glass is continually refilled, and you get to catch up on the latest neighborhood gossip. Husbands are also invited to these playdates— they're the designated drivers.

Playdates in a Pinch. You're about to close the biggest deal of a lifetime when suddenly your cell phone starts buzzing in your suit pocket. You fumble for the phone and your megawatt smile instantly fades as your baby-sitter informs you she has to leave immediately to take her six-year-old to the doctor.

You know you can't reach your husband because he's working late, too, and your mother-in-law has dinner plans with her colorist.

Who can you call? That's simple: the most reliable and by far the coolest mom in town who doesn't mind picking up your tots, bringing them to her house, and serving them a well-balanced dinner. Big shout-out to the moms who've been there for us in a pinch—without you, our cats would be baby-sitting our kids. (Just joking, we're not that nuts. Cats can't figure out how to stick a straw into a juice box or work the DVD player.)

Palatial Playdates. Let's be honest. These are, hands down, our favorite kind of play-date. Who doesn't want to check out that gorgeous center hall colonial down the street that you've had your eye on since you moved into the neighborhood? Going on a palatial playdate is just like going to a real estate open house but you don't have to worry about leaving a fake name and address because you know you can't afford to buy anything.

We admit it, sometimes we are the prover-bial nosy neighbors, or as we like to call ourselves, the decorating detectives. We'll jump at the chance to check out the home of our new neighbor who just moved into the McMansion down the road. "Of course, Rebecca would love to come by and swim in your gunite swimming pool . . . no, we don't have any other plans," as you quickly pick up your cell phone to cancel a playdate with the Peculiars.

Mentally taking note as you walk into the grand entrance hall, you marvel at the expansive floor plan, admiring everything from the dentil crown molding to the marble mantels to the custom made mahogany cabinetry.

Unfortunately, our kids can sometimes sabotage our interior investigations before we've even had a chance to check out the master suite. In one memorable mansion, Beth's daughter launched into a screaming fit with her three-year-old hostess, fighting over toys and pretty much ruining the playdate before Beth even had a chance to finish counting all the bathrooms.

Role Mommy
Reality Check

Be careful what you wish for. Dialing up a playdate may seem like a quick fix for your busy life and your bored kids, but proceed with caution. Make sure your child's companion has the pedigree of a UN Peacekeeper. Once the tables are turned, the last thing you want to do is host a devious troublemaker from down the street who manages to find the only markers in your house that aren't washable and decides to graffiti your playroom walls with the memorable phrase: Timmy wuz here.

OUR LIVES...
B.C. before children
and
after diapers A.D.

Just Desserts

B.C. The satisfaction you finally feel at your ten-year high school reunion when you glance over to see your old boyfriend and that two-bit hussy who stole him away by letting him go all the way. Your former lover boy is now a loser. He's bald and fat and you can't help but giggle as you overhear him complaining about how he hasn't had sex since his mother-in-law moved in a year ago.

A.D. The only time you can get your kids to sit still at a table for more than 10 minutes at a time. To really put your brood into sugar shock, you order up a round of gummy bears and Oreos mixed into a huge mound of rocky road ice cream.

10

The Cupcake Question

I T'S TIME for a cooking quiz.
When your child is sick, do you.

A. Grab the nearest can opener and crack open a can of Campbell's.
B. Slowly simmer a free-range chicken for several hours, adding vegetables and rice, and serve up a bowl of piping hot chicken soup.

Unlike the quizzes you remember from high school, there are no right or wrong answers to this one—just some very different ways that moms deal with meals.

You're either a sous chef, Sara Lee, or maybe, somewhere in between. For us, it's pretty clean cut. Plain and simple, Yvette cooks and Beth makes reservations. When you're a mom, it all comes down to the cupcake question—do you or don't you?

I Don't Do Cupcakes

Beth's Story

LET THE record show . . . I don't do cupcakes. I also don't do homemade cakes, pies, or cookies either. I've got no problems with munchkins, Entenmann's, or Freihoffers, but please, spare me the drama from mothers who lament that they stayed up all hours of the night baking for a big school event.

Just the other day I was waiting to pick up my daughter from school and the conversation began like it always does. "What are you baking for the class tomorrow?"

"Oh, I'm making vanilla cupcakes with chocolate frosting," said one PTA mom.

"I'm baking cookies, and I plan to prepare enough for the class and perhaps the entire school," the competition piped up.

All I could think to myself was, I hope I can make it to Dunkin Donuts in time to get some decent munchkins. As long as I can get some chocolates, jellies, and some white powdered ones and still get back to the school in time for my daughter's class performance, I'll be sitting pretty.

The next day I came prepared. As I walked down the aisle of the auditorium to claim my front row seat, I had my munchkin box by my side (chocolate, jellies, and powdered neatly tucked away), and I saw my friend Robin, a fellow working mom with an equally hectic and harried schedule holding a lovely basket full of goodies.

Upon further inspection, I was quite pleased to find that much like myself, Robin had totally migrated over to the no-nonsense side of motherhood. No homemade cupcakes on display—just tasty individually wrapped Hostess chocolate cupcakes, lovingly displayed in a basket that she found on a desperate search the night before. The results were safe, sanitary, and tasty—in a word, priceless.

As a working mother, I try not to sweat the cupcakes. Maybe it's because I spend all day at work sweating out the culinary needs of others—for example, an actor who stares disapprovingly at my chocolate-brown suede suit while announcing he's a vegan. While pampering my celebrity guests and keeping straight who's a Zoner, a South Beacher, or a Weight Watcher and who lives on Jolly Ranchers, I find myself jumping through hoops to make sure everyone's happy. By the time I get home to my own kids, the last place I want to be is elbow deep in icing and burnt muffin tins.

Sure I get disapproving stares from the moms who have slaved away making custom designed cupcakes that are color coordinated for special events—like the mother who concocted cupcakes with orange icing for Halloween that went untouched, and then she took another stab at it with Pepto Bismol colored cookies for Valentine's Day. The effort, I admit, was valiant—the results, not so delectable.

If I wanted to pursue a career as Mrs. Fields then I'm sure I would be baking to my heart's content, but you know what? Those enterprising bakers do it better than me.

Here's my philosophy on the cupcake brigade—if you can't beat 'em, buy 'em.

Besides, if you ever took a mental note of what is actually eaten at school events, nine times out of ten, kids go for the store-bought food; it's tried and true, and it tastes better.

So moms, if you're thinking of pulling an all-nighter on a Betty Crocker expedition, try something more productive, like sleep. Then the next morning while you're multitasking, take your gas guzzler for a $90 fill up and zip inside the Quickie Mart so you can snatch up a box of chocolate chip Nabiscos for class cookie day.

One little footnote to my cupcake tirade. Although I don't do cupcakes, I do make matzoh balls. The reason—it's what my Grandma Dora taught me to make for Passover and what I want to pass on to my children. I still recall standing by her side while I rolled the balls and she dropped them in the boiling water. The memories are still fresh in my mind to this day.

So why compete with the queens of confection? Better stick with what you know best, and what I know is how to purchase baked goods and make a mean matzoh ball soup.

Beth's Matzoh Ball Recipe

Buy box of Streit's or Manischewitz Matzoh
     Ball Mix.
Follow directions.
Add a capful of seltzer for buoyancy.
After mixing ingredients, stick the bowl in the
     fridge.
Wait 15 minutes.
Take out the bowl, have your child roll the
     balls (after washing his or her hands)
     and give them back to you so that you
     can drop them in boiling water.
Watch your matzoh balls grow.
After 5–10 minutes, take them out and drop
     them in your soup.

SOUP
Use store-bought Streit's or Manischewitz
     soup mix that accompanies the matzoh
     ball packet.
Add kosher chicken.
Add carrots.
Add celery.
Drop in a few onions.
Throw in some parsley.

Toss in some salt and pepper (not too little, not too much).
Cover the pot and simmer for a few hours.

Mazel Tov . . . you have just made matzoh balls and soup!

I Do Do Cupcakes

Yvette's Story

I'm a shiksa who's never made matzoh ball soup. I'm a Greek woman who grew up with spanakopita, baklava, and souvlaki. My mother was home to make dinner for us every single night—she didn't work outside of the home. Raising, feeding, and caring for her children was her job. Now, over thirty years later, after a long day at work, I head home to my two children, my husband, and my pots and pans. I, like my mother, feel the need to feed. You see, I *do* do cupcakes—and quiche and coq au vin and a considerable few other few things. You've heard of the galloping gourmet? Well, meet the guilty gourmet.

Yes, that's me. Television producer by day. Producer of over-the-top meals for family and friends by night—and sometimes early mornings too.

Although I would never dream of turning the pursuit for the perfect baked goods into a blue ribbon bake off, I must 'fess up, I'm overjoyed when the PTA president or even the playdate du jour salivates over my latest culinary creation.

I may not be the perfect suburban mom. My closets are always a mess, and even at the end of the school year, I still don't know the names of all the children in my daughter's class, but, when it comes to cooking, now there's an area where I can compete.

No, for me cupcakes won't do. It has to be exotic, special. I'll be up until midnight whipping up a feast for four-year-olds . . . butterfly cupcakes, banana bread, peanut butter chocolate chip cookies, coconut custard, carrot cake with cream cheese frosting, and every kind of homemade ice cream you can imagine.

But why stop at the bake sale? With birthday parties, barbecues, and family dinners to plan, I can slave over five courses and cook for three days. And after working fifty hours, commuting two hours per day, and chasing after two children in my spare time, doesn't that sound like fun?

It's an illness. It's warped. I have a code-pendent relationship with my kitchen.

I know I'm trying to make up for lost time. I know that the homemade pizza, meatloaf, chicken tenders, and soup in the fridge won't fill the void that I left when I left my children asleep in their beds this morning. Let's face it, the only one these comfort foods are comforting is me.

But I can't tell you what joy it gives me when I call to check in and the baby-sitter tells me the kids have devoured the whole-wheat panko-crusted chicken tenders I left for them. So what if I had to check three stores to find the right breadcrumbs? So what if I spend my Saturday shopping around for the freshest antibiotic and hormone-free chicken tenders instead of hitting the gym? And so what if I made the fire alarm go off (again) as I fried them in extra virgin olive oil?

And then, there are the bunny burgers. My greatest accomplishment in life is the creation of the bunny burger. There is nothing more gratifying for a mother (working or not) than to find something, preferably nutritious, that you can add to your finicky eater's oh-so-limited repertoire.

For me, the bunny burger was born out of sheer frustration. I could not allow my daughter to continue living on ice cream, corn on the cob, and pizza. As a Greek woman, raising chubby babies is in my genetic makeup. I had come to terms with the fact that Christiana would never have a single roll of delicious baby fat on her body—but I couldn't let her starve to death. And so, the bunny burger was born.

After yet another marathon session reading *Guess How Much I Love You?*, I retired to the kitchen—the dread of dinnertime once again upon me. Oh God, do I have to feed her again? Then it hit me: make it fun and make it what she loves. Make it a bunny. After frying up some turkey meat with a magic mixture of ingredients, carrots for the ears, cauliflower for the tail, and broccoli for the nose, the bunny burger was born. She devoured it and has done so ever since.

But kids cannot live on bunny burgers alone. I, like every other mother, have a serious urge to see my kids suck down some spinach. And again, here's where my Greekness comes out. Spanakopita, or spinach pie, is a staple of the Greek diet and a fantastic way to get kids to eat those leafy greens that everyone is always gushing about. But if you've ever made a recipe that requires the use of filo, you know how difficult and time-consuming it can be to work with those paper thin sheets of dough. And for a time-strapped working mom, it can be an absolute nightmare. So finally, after many Saturday afternoons spent fighting with the delicate filo dough required for perfect spanakopita, I finally figured out an easy way to make a relatively hassle free spinach pie that's fun for the kids to eat as well as easy to assemble. My secret weapons are cookie cutters and ready made pie crust. I simply roll out the pie crust and use the kids' favorite cookie cutters to cut out top and bottom crusts. I drop a dollop of the super healthy spinach filling inside and bake until they're golden brown. The kids love eating these cute petite pies and I love putting a modern spin on a Greek classic.

But why stop there? Why rest on my laurels? Why be content to have created something special? Oh no, that's never enough. I live in a constant state of top *that.*

I cannot count the number of times that I've happily, gladly, willingly, and giddily volunteered to cook or cater for a party. Mais oui, baked brie to start, shrimp dumplings sound divine, I've been told my bouillabaisse is the best, and for dessert, would you like café with your crème brulee? I love the shopping, the cooking, the serving, the savoring, in short, the whole creative process.

But, once the feast is over, belts are unbuckled, and diets are dissolved, that's when the high of cooking fades and I come crashing back to reality. I hate the mess, I hate the cleanup, I hate scrubbing the pots, and I hate the gunk that's left in the sink when all that disgusting water drains. I hate it.

Right about the time that my guests are sipping their last few drops of coffee, the hatred starts to ferment and the bitterness seeps in and oozes all over my kitchen. It works its way like a sticky film all over the wedding china I swore to my mother I would never put in the dishwasher and the crystal bowls I foolishly used for the side dishes. It careens across the kitchen, covers every glass, platter, and serving plate, and then, it ricochets off the range and comes to rest on my guests.

What's the matter with these people? How can they just sit there sipping their drinks without a care in the world? Haven't they seen the pile of crusty crap in the kitchen? What the hell is wrong with her? Why can't she pick up a Brillo pad and start scrubbing? What do they think this is, a restaurant? Don't they know I have to get up and go to work in the morning?

You would think that I would have learned my lesson by now—that I would learn to make a dozen plain chocolate cupcakes for the bake sale or a simple dinner for friends instead of a four course feast.

No such luck. The more I work, the more I want to make it up to my family. The more extravagant the meal, the messier the kitchen, and inevitably, the worse the cleanup. But such is the life of a guilty gourmet as I try to bake, sizzle, fry, and sauté my guilt away.

Panko Crusted Chicken Tenders

1 package chicken tenders
    *You can use breast meat but it's tougher
    and drier—discerning pint-sized palates
    usually prefer the tenders
1 cup flour
3 eggs
2 cups whole wheat panko breadcrumbs
1/2 cup olive oil

Rinse the tenders and pat dry with a paper
    towel.
Place flour in a shallow pan and dredge the
    tenders in the flour.
Beat the eggs in a small bowl.
Dip the flour-dredged tenders into the eggs.
Take the panko breadcrumbs and place
    them into a shallow pan. Place the egg-
    washed tenders into the breadcrumbs
    and turn them until they are completely
    covered.
Heat the olive oil in a skillet. Cook thoroughly
    over medium heat.

Bunny Burgers

1 pound ground turkey meat
2 eggs
½ cup olive oil
½ cup Italian seasoned bread crumbs
Carrots, broccoli, cauliflower or any other
vegetables you have on hand

In a large bowl, mix ground turkey meat,
eggs, bread crumbs, and 2 tablespoons
olive oil.

Coat a frying pan with 3 tablespoons of olive
oil. Take about 2 heaping tablespoons of
the mixture and use your hands to mold
a large meatball. Flatten in your palm
until it looks like a giant circle. Use your
fingers to indent the top of the circle and
shape like two bunny ears. Cook thoroughly over medium heat and transfer
to a plate.

*This makes enough for about 6 bunny
burgers. You can freeze the unused
turkey meat mixture.

Take your veggies and start decorating.

2 baby carrots for the ears.

Cauliflower for the eyes and teeth.

Broccoli for the nose.

*Feel free to improvise the veggies—whatever you have on hand will work. Kids love to do the decorating themselves. For those bunny hating older kids, brontosaurus burgers work just as well. Who cares what they call it—as long as they eat it!

Silly Spanakopita

1½ cups loosely packed fresh spinach leaves
2 eggs
¼ cup feta cheese
¼ cup ricotta cheese
1 package prepared pie crust
½ cup water

Cookie cutters—use what you like, but the larger the shape, the easier it is to fill and work with. Also, simple, clean lines like hearts are easy to work with, whereas more intricate shapes like gingerbread men will be more difficult to fill and seal.

Depending on the size and shape of the cookie cutters, you may have extra filling or pie crust. There's no right or wrong shape or size for these, just choose what you think your kids will chow down on.

In a medium sized bowl, combine the spinach, 1 egg, feta, and ricotta cheese. Mix well.

Roll out the pie dough and cut out your cookie cutter shapes.

Each pie requires 2 shapes. Place the first shape on a nonstick cookie sheet. Place a dollop of the filling in the center of the cookie shape and flatten with a spoon. You want to spread the filling across the cookie shape without going all the way to the edge. Dip your finger in the water and wet the edge of the dough all along the cookie shape. Place the second cookie shape on top and use a fork to press the edges of the cookies together in order to properly seal.

In a small bowl or cup, combine one egg and 3 tablespoons of water. Beat until frothy, and use a pastry brush to coat each pie with this egg wash mixture.

Bake at 375 degrees for about 20 minutes, or until golden brown.

Role Mommy
Reality Check

Whether you're a butcher, a baker, or a cupcake maker, the only thing that matters is that you're spending time with your children. Love to cook? Great! Invite your kids into the kitchen and together you'll put Chef Boyardee to shame. And if your forte is takeout, then take your kids along for an outing to your favorite cupcake café. Involve your kids in the process. It doesn't matter how you do it. Making memories is the perfect recipe.

OUR LIVES...
B.C. before children
and
after diapers A.D.

Escort Service

B.C. The upscale stripper service your soon-to-be husband's best man hired for his bachelor party.

A.D. You, the one-woman escort service for a toddler who has just been potty trained. Every time you're about to sit down on the couch, head to the kitchen, get in the car, or enjoy your meal at a restaurant, you're immediately called into action the moment your preschool pimp calls out your name.

11

Our Lives as Groupies: From Wham to the Wiggles

REMEMBER WHEN George Michael was straight and you were going to marry him and have his babies? Actually, it was a toss-up between George Michael from Wham and Simon Lebon from Duran Duran, but everybody wanted to marry Simon so you figured your chances were better with George.

Ah yes, to be a child of the 1980s—groupie heaven. There were so many great hair bands to obsess over.

When we were teenagers it was all about the connections. Who had connections was the hottest topic of conversation. It was always some obscure sixth degree of separation thing: my cousin's friend's sister's aunt knows some guy who says his brother works for Flock of Seagulls, and she says they're gonna hook us up with some tickets . . . maybe even back-stage passes.

"Oh my God, what are you going to wear?"

Now, those days are long behind us, even though Duran Duran keeps insisting on touring every few years, bringing all those painful memories rushing back to us.

Today, with an Outlook address book brimming with contacts, we've managed to call many of those coveted connections our own. But there's no need to fight for front row seats or call in any favors when your favorite bands are now headlining at Atlantic City's own Trump Taj Mahal Casino.

So, who is playing Madison Square Garden and Radio City, you ask? The creatures, char-acters, and cartoons made famous by the Disney Channel and Nickelodeon, that's who. Just when you thought your groupie days were behind you, here comes yet another reason to start wrangling for those backstage passes: our kids. Or so we say.

Let's be real for a moment, shall we? Will our children really know if Dora comes exploring in our town and we don't take them to see her? Is catching Snow White on ice really worth $100 per ticket? And do we really have to scalp tickets for Pokemon at the Paramount? The answers are no.

But, admit it, once a groupie, always a groupie. You can't resist the thrill of the hunt, scoring those tickets for the latest kid's cult phenomenon no matter the cost. As they say, admitting you have a problem is the first step. Yvette admits she had one hell of a problem on her hands when the Wiggles and their Big Red Car rolled into town.

Yvette and The Wiggles: A Love/Hate Story

IT ALL started with a favor. In 2001, I was producing a news and entertainment show on WCBS called *New York Live.* I picked up the phone one day to hear one of my favorite publicists, Katie Schroeder of Radio City Music Hall, pitching a segment on this great, but still relatively unknown, Australian children's group called The Wiggles. The last thing I wanted to do was book some goofy-looking group of guys who sang about fruit salad and mashed potatoes. But Katie was a great contact and my one-stop-shopping access to booking a kick line with the Rockettes and Santa every holiday season, so I felt I owed her and agreed to book the unknowns from Down Under.

The day finally arrived and the Wiggles showed up in the studio. All I can remember thinking is wow, I feel really sorry for these guys. I bet they're all frustrated out-of-work actors who just can't catch a break and decided to try the kids' party circuit for a change. Here were four grown men walking around my studio looking ridiculous in their color-coordinated costumes with these goofy grins on their faces and actually wiggling every time they introduced themselves. I was completely embarrassed for them and annoyed with myself for caving in and putting them on the air.

As for the Wiggles, they could not have been nicer—laughing, joking with the crew, and so completely grateful for being given exposure on American television. Katie and the Wiggles left that day thanking me up and down for giving them some airtime. I left the studio that day swearing never again to do any favors that involved grown men making fools of themselves, and so openly enjoying themselves, as they sang about mashed bananas and cold spaghetti. That was my life B.C. (before children).

Fast-forward three years and I'm once again face to face with the Wiggles. This time, however, it's not in the studio and I'm not the producer. No, this time they're in my living room, den, kitchen, car, and even bedroom. This time I'm a mother of a two-year-old girl who is obsessed with the goofy group of guys I reluctantly put on television a few years back. Now I no longer think they're goofy. I think they're gods. Christiana actually sits still long enough to watch them make that damn fruit salad, and you would think that batch of mashed potatoes would have gone bad by now, but no, her little fingers are mashing right along with theirs.

At this point in my life, I had stopped working full time and was working as a freelance producer. It was the dead of summer so there wasn't much work out there. I found myself spending more and more time fighting with my toddler and less and less time fighting with the paparazzi. I quickly realized that a toddler was a much tougher opponent than even the wildest pack of European photographers imported in for fashion week.

In my battle-scarred state of facing off with the terrible twos, a child who still wouldn't sleep through the night, and the realization that I may never work or see my friends or the inside of a gym again, the unthinkable happened. I remember looking at the television while Christiana danced along with Greg, Murray, Anthony, and Jeff. In my lonely, exhausted, overwhelmed, and starved for adult interaction state, I remember staring at the television and thinking, hey, the one in the blue T-shirt, that Anthony guy, is really hot.

It was a cry for help and I heard it loud and clear. You know you are moving into dangerous territory when you have the hots for the Wiggles. Within days, I was on the phone desperately looking for work and lining up playdates for myself.

I finally got past my Anthony fixation, but the Wiggles weren't out of my life just yet. Christiana was still obsessed when the Wiggles came to town in 2004. Out came the Rolodex; it was time to cash in on some favors from the past. I was lucky enough to score four prime seats for the Wiggles for the bargain basement price of close to $400.

Yes, there is something very, very wrong with this picture.

And just like any really good groupie story—this one wraps up with a warped little ending. Sometimes Karma's a bitch, and sometimes, like in this case, she just has an incredible sense of humor.

Who ever would have thought that after pouring my heart out and sharing my embarrassing kiddie crush in the first edition of this book for all the world to read and ridicule that it would happen. Yes, six years after our initial meeting, I once again came face to face with the object of my fantasies and affection. I, television producer and mother of two, was sent on assignment to cover the Wiggles. I've never moved so fast in my life, snatching a copy of this book off my desk, grabbing my press pass, and running out the door before anyone dared to change my assignment.

As always, the boys were the consummate professionals, answering my questions with sincerity and smiles. This was just as Greg, everyone's favorite yellow, left the group because of an illness, so I got to meet the new Wiggle, along with all of our old favorites. And there, right in the middle of it all, separated from me merely by my microphone, was Anthony.

What can I say? He was as handsome and charming as ever. Now, at this point in my life, I really do think I've made great strides, I have a strong grip on reality, and I've even stopped fantasizing about being his backup dancer. I held it together and conducted my interview with the guys, but there was no way in hell I was going to let this perfect opportunity pass me by. I pulled out a copy of *Peeing in Peace* and I spilled my guts for all the Wiggles to hear. Did they think I was nuts? Maybe. Did they agree to pose for a picture with me? Absolutely. Did I make sure

I snuggled right up in there next to Anthony? You bet your ass!

OK, so maybe our little encounter sent me momentarily back down the scary and slippery slope of Wiggle worship. But you know what, who cares?

At least I can sit back now and laugh at how in just a few short years I transformed from producer to pathetic groupie. Even though I may slip up again, I do think for the most part I've got it all in check. But, in all honesty, that brilliant white smile and that sexy little Aussie accent still makes me swoon just a bit.

Role Mommy
Reality Check

I will not spend ridiculous amounts of money for tickets to an over-the-top kiddie show. I'd rather stick my husband and three of his friends in Red, Blue, Yellow, and Green T-shirts to perform *Hot Potato* at my son's next birthday party. Trust us, kids under four don't know the difference. Five year olds . . . that's a different story, but by the time they reach kindergarten, they're Wiggle free and have moved into Cheetah Girls territory. So save your cash and be creative when your kids are young. We promise, your ten-month-old won't be scarred for life if she misses seeing "Barney at the Beacon" this time around. Take her to the park to feed the ducks instead—she'll find the real life animals a lot more amusing than the sweaty guy on stage who can't wait to get out of his uncomfortably itchy purple suit.

OUR LIVES...
B.C. before children
and
after diapers A.D.

Space Invaders

B.C. That addictive 1980s video game you played with your older brother. He'd always beat the pants off of you so you'd ditch him for a few rounds of Ms. Pacman.

A.D. Preschoolers who invade your personal space at every turn. These itty bitty invaders insist on sitting on your lap at a restaurant just as your entree arrives and even barge in on you in the bathroom stall as you pull your thong up from around your ankles, loudly demanding, "Mommy, I want a prize from that thingamajig on the wall!" Unfortunately for them, the prize comes in two varieties: tampon or sanitary napkin.

12

The Home Team

OUR LIVES as expert jugglers would not be possible without the support of what we'd like to call the home team. You may have the perfect nanny who's been a part of your life since your kids were infants; your mom lives around the corner and is always there in a pinch if your child upchucks at school; your best friend pitches in when you're out at a late night conference; and let's not forget your sister, brother, next door neighbor, the teen baby-sitter from down the street, and last, but never least, your husband.

All of these people play an important role in helping you manage the juggle. Without them, the jigsaw puzzle that is your life would probably be missing a few pieces.

Think about it, even the most buttoned-up type A mom has to admit that she needs a little help now and then. Scientists may have found a way to clone sheep, but they're still lagging far behind in the mommy department. We all know it's physically impossible to be in two places at once, so let go of that white-knuckled control freak grip and head straight to your bullpen where you can find yourself a great middle reliever.

Welcome to Camp Feldman

I AM pleased to report that my husband is a child at heart. I never really enjoyed relay or potato sack races, but my husband has become a master at devising elaborate schemes for my kids to have a ball right in their own backyard.

While I'm in charge of cooking and clean-up, Darin is the director of fun. After returning home from a long day at the office, I rush to decide what culinary monstrosity I'll be whipping up that evening while my husband takes the kids outside for a game of wiffle ball and backyard sprints.

When the weather gets brisk, he takes the routine indoors, where he's devised an ingenious hundred-penny obstacle course (touch a penny with your toe and you lose) and has hosted marathon hangman sessions that have lasted until bedtime.

After I slip the kids into their pajamas and convince them to brush their teeth, Darin launches into story time, where he creates original adventures for their amusement. I've been so thoroughly entertained by his Leo, Max, and Nigel tale about three zoo animals who take my son on a trip through the park that I've even taken creative license to retell the story when Darin's been off duty at a late night dinner. I, of course, offer a slightly different twist—sending Leo, Max, and Nigel along with my kids on a vacation to see their grandparents in Boynton Beach, Florida. Unfortunately, Grandpa Neil sends the trio off to the zoo to bunk with their relatives because Grandma won't allow smelly animals in the house.

I think Darin has become so wrapped up in playtime because he spent his early years in beauty parlors and nail salons. You see, his mom, who was single at the time, took him wherever she went. Unfortunately, when it was time for her monthly dye job, Darin got a crash course in tinting and coloring. So today, he's an amazing and involved Dad who gets to relive his childhood through our children.

My husband is truly my other half—he zigs when I zag and he plays like a school kid while I pick up after everyone. The two of us make a great team and I wouldn't want to have it any other way.

Our Very Own Family Circus— Beware of Greeks Bearing Gifts in Toys R Us Bags

Yvette's Story

MY HUSBAND Dave and I share the same philosophy on child care—for us, it's a family affair.

It's because of this shared philosophy that Dave and I did the unthinkable back when Christiana turned one. We, the ultimate urban-ites, decided to, gulp, sell our treasured classic Brooklyn Heights apartment and make the move to suburbia. WHAT????!!! Our friends couldn't believe that we were giving up our chic address and subway lifestyle to move to the land of lawn mowers and Land Rovers.

Here's what it came down to: we really didn't want to hire a stranger to watch our precious baby. When I got a freelance gig and was called into action, I'd call on my mother, Kiki, to come watch the baby. If I was booked for one day of work she would leave her Westchester home at the ungodly hour of 4 a.m. so she could drive to Brooklyn in time for me to leave for work. Or, if I was booked for a few days, she'd pack a bag and move in until my gig was up.

Kiki never once complained about her exhausting excursions to Brooklyn because she loved caring for Christiana. But Dave and I started to feel guilty about the situation and reality finally set in that we'd either have to hire a nanny or move so we could be closer to our built-in baby-sitting service.

So, we did it. We found a house conveniently located approximately ten minutes from my parents, and inconveniently located around the block from Toys R Us.

Whereas the move made it possible for my mother to continue caring for her Christiana and now naughty Nico, too, it also allowed the rest of the family to join the child care family circus.

Our proximity to Toys R Us made it easier for my father, Tasso, and my brother, Emanuel, to relish their roles as the primary spoilers in our family. At least once a week, you can spot each of them pulling up to the house with shopping bags in hand—sending the kids into a Toys R Us induced frenzy.

It got so bad that at one point my home became the last stop on the all night party patrol for my brother and his drunken friends. You could set your watch by them. Every Sunday morning at 6 a.m., my brother and his buddies would pull up to our house, windows rolled down and Dean Martin or Frank Sinatra blaring from the stereo. My neighbors didn't exactly appreciate the early morning wakeup call, but I never minded because one or both of the kids inevitably had me up and on my second cup of coffee by that time anyway. Emanuel and his motley crew would saunter in, gift bags in hand, or sometimes it was a bag of donuts from the all night coffee shop if they didn't have time to hit the toy store before their night out. On the rare occasions that Emanuel would show up empty handed, he'd pass out on the couch for a few hours until Toys R Us opened for business at 11a.m. How he got any sleep I have no idea, with the kids continually poking at him every five minutes asking, "Is Toys R Us open yet?"

At first we fought it and asked my family to cease and desist with these spoiling shopping trips. But finally, we gave in. Isn't that what grandparents and uncles are for anyway, to spoil our kids with attention and the mess-making finger paints set that we would never spring for?

As for child care, we did eventually hire a part-time nanny to make the things a little easier for my mother. In keeping with the family circus theme, we allowed her to bring her baby daughter along so she didn't have to worry about finding child care herself.

After two years together, our nanny left to raise her own growing family. Once more faced with the "to nanny or not" question—we have again opted out. Instead, Dave has adjusted his work schedule. He now works weekends and is home during the week to play part-time Mr. Mom.

Am I bummed about not having a shared day off with my husband? Of course I am. Am I going out of my mind because I'm flying solo and there's no one to help me when Nico decides to dive bomb from the couch onto his sister's head? Are you kidding me? Would I give just about anything for an hour alone so I could use the treadmill that's collecting dust in my basement? What do you think?

Are the sacrifices worth it? Absolutely.

Sometimes, when you have kids, you've got to take one for the team.

Let's Do the Wave for Our Heavy Hitters—A Grand Salute to Grandma

THE WORDS "just wait until you're a mother" made you cringe when you were a teenager, but now that you have children of your own, you finally get it. It's time to acknowledge that mother does know best after all. No, it's not just because the tables have turned and you now must do battle with your own daughter. But, as a grown woman with a family of your own, you sometimes find yourself thinking more than ever, "I want my mommy!"

So come clean, swallow your pride, and tell your mother you're sorry for throwing the tantrum of the century when she dragged you to the beauty parlor to cut off your knot-filled hair for a Dorothy Hamill or little Dutch Boy bob. Beg her forgiveness for being such a teen terror and admit that maybe getting an ankle tattoo with the name of your prom date on it wasn't the greatest idea in the world. And fess up to that keg party you threw while she was out of town that left a mysterious stain on the living room rug that you blamed on the Shih Tzu. It's about time you tell your mom how much you love and need her.

No one loves your kids like Grandma does. And there's no one more willing to spend their weekends baby sitting so you can actually go out and have an adult dinner for a change. So whether you're a Granny, Nana, Bubbe, or Ya Ya, just know that we love you, appreciate all that you do, and by the way, if you're available, we need you this Saturday night!

Help Wanted: Mary Poppins, Where Are You?

FORGET THE fountain of youth, a day at the spa, or a killer wardrobe. Ask any working mother and she'll tell you that the holy grail doesn't come from a bottle, boutique, or beauty parlor. Today's busy moms are striving for something far more precious and rare—the perfect nanny.

Wouldn't it be great if she flew in one windy day with umbrella in hand and landed on your doorstep? Then she'd whip the kids into shape, instructing them on the finer points of folding laundry, how to eat broccoli and not gag, and how to make their beds, military style. Mary Poppins, where are you and how much do you charge per hour?

Whether it's through the local Pennysaver, a referral agency, or word of mouth, when you stumble upon your personal version of Ms. Poppins, you, my friend, have hit the nanny lottery. Do whatever you can to keep her happy because, trust us, other moms are lurking in the shadows, ready to steal her away. If you're lucky enough to find someone who makes your children happy, cares for them, and loves them like her own, then Mary Poppins need not apply. Not only have you found an amazing caregiver, but you have gained a wonderful new member of your family, too.

Everyone Needs an Auntie Mame

EVERYONE KNOWS being a mother is the hardest job known to mankind—okay, maybe rocket science is really the toughest job on the planet, but motherhood is a pretty close second. Now, if you're a single mom, hats off to you, you're probably working twice as hard. You deserve a standing ovation and an all-expense paid week at Canyon Ranch—alone.

For the single mom, it's even more difficult to carve out time for yourself. That's why it's even more crucial to rely on someone you trust who can step in at a moment's notice and watch your kids while you're out late at a last minute meeting or on a date with a hot prospect.

Our dear friend and single mom, Cindy Hsu, amazes us. Cindy is a news anchor for WCBS-TV in New York. She's smart, successful, and always knew that she wanted to be a mother. So when Mr. Right failed to show up in a timely fashion, Cindy took matters into her own hands. She traveled to China and adopted a beautiful baby girl who she named Rosie.

It's tough to find a business that is more demanding than television news. There is no such thing as a holiday or weekend. There's an old newsroom saying "news never sleeps." Well, it's true, and those who work in news never sleep either. Forget how glamorous all those anchors look (and Cindy always looks glamorous). Forget the hair and makeup and wardrobe and think about the work for a moment. The next time you turn over in bed and grab the remote at 7 a.m. to get your fix of morning news, think about the anchor who is giving you your morning headlines. That nattily dressed newsreader schlepped herself to the office at 3 a.m. to prepare for the show. Not so glamorous anymore, right? And not so easy if you're a single mom who needs a great child care provider who doesn't mind waking up before dawn to step in when you need to step out in front of the cameras.

So, what does Cindy do? Call on her friends, of course. Cindy has an arsenal of friends just waiting in the wings to watch Rosie. There are the single friends who practice their parenting skills on Rosie and dream of the day that they, too, will have children of their own. There are the older friends who've already raised their kids, but to them, being around Rosie is like a beautiful blast from the past. And there are all of the amazing Auntie Mames ready to pitch in with Rosie when Cindy's crazy schedule calls for her to be away from home.

Sure Cindy misses her baby, don't we all? But Rosie's having the time of her life surrounded by the incredible extended family Cindy has created for her, people who lavish her with love and attention while mommy's out in Weehawken covering a water main break.

Role Mommy
Reality Check

Without the support of a strong home team, you could be setting yourself up for a strike out. So make sure that when you become a mom, you work extra hard to assemble a great lineup. In the end, you'll not only cover all your bases but will also strike the balance you've been searching for.

OUR LIVES...
B.C. before children
and
after diapers A.D.

Guilt Trip

B.C. How your mom would make you feel if you didn't want to attend the out-of-town wedding of your third cousin twice removed.

A.D. A business trip that takes you away from your kids and your husband for three days straight. You miss the kids terribly and feel bad about leaving them home. The guilt seeps in even deeper as you think about your husband having to handle bedtime battles all alone. Then, it happens. You sink into that king-sized bed with the goose down pillows and the guilt fades away just long enough for a good night's sleep—but then it comes right back the next morning when your kids call to say, "We miss you, Mommy."

13

Give Yourself a Time-Out!

CONGRATULATIONS. YOU'VE done it. You've figured out a way to carve out time for your career and your kids.

So your boss thinks you're the bomb, your children are charming and well-behaved, and your girlfriends are insanely jealous that you've found a way to straddle both worlds so beautifully. Yes, you are a marvel of modern motherhood.

Now, before you get all smug, Superwoman, wipe that smile off your face and answer a few questions. You're not out of the woods just yet.

- When was the last time you had a night out with your girlfriends?
- When was the last time you had a facial or a massage, or really indulged yourself with something special?
- When was the last time you had a date with your significant other?
- When was the last time you had sex?
- When was the last time you had great sex?

In a perfect world, you've done all of these things at least once in the past month, and some three or four times, at least.

In reality, you might have done two or three of these things in the past month.

There's still hope for you if you've done one of these things in the past month.

If you've done NONE of these things in the past month, you are in need of an immediate intervention.

We know you run around all day making sure that everything and everyone else is taken care of—from your colleagues to your kids and everyone in between. But come on, you're a mother not a martyr! You need to have a little fun now and then—with your friends, your spouse, battery operated objects, whatever! All work and no play not only makes for a dull life but it's also a recipe for disaster that can inevitably send you hurtling down the freeway on a crash course toward Farbissina Punim Syndrome.

The Farbissina Punim Syndrome

IF YOU'RE not Jewish, this is also commonly referred to as the Martyr Syndrome. If you are Jewish, you're smiling because you've gotten the joke and can probably relate. A Farbissina Punim is someone who is a sourpuss. But not just any sourpuss, think of the most miserable, unhappy, negative, horror to be around, nothing positive to say, face all scrunched up like you're constipated, pain in the butt pessimist.

Get the picture?

If it's been a while since you've had a date night or pedicure or you can't remember the last time you laughed so hard with your girlfriends you almost peed in your pants, then you are a prime candidate for Farbissina Punim Syndrome.

The cure for this all too common ailment is simple. Give yourself a time-out. Only this time-out has nothing to do with sitting on a step, unless of course you plan on having sex on it.

Time-outs can take on many forms, but they have one thing in common: they're meant to make you rediscover and remember who you are—you, yes, YOU. Not the mother or the career girl—you, the woman.

So get out there, get a baby-sitter, forget about the unfolded laundry, and don't even think of starting those status reports your boss has been bugging you about.

Instead, it's time to reignite your passion, rekindle your romance, and reconnect with your girlfriends.

The Mating Game

WHEN YOU first met your spouse, could you not keep your hands off each other? Did you hold hands all the time? Did you get those crazy butterflies in your stomach just at the thought of kissing him?

Now fast-forward five, ten, or even fifteen years. You're both a little round around the edges, you popped out a few kids, and the spark between you definitely seems to have dimmed. Well, from here on out, it's time to get back your mojo and rustle up the bed sheets! No matter how tired you are after putting the kids to bed, or even in those pre-dawn hours when you're relishing the last fifteen minutes before the alarm clock sounds, you still need to make time for the stuff that got you pregnant in the first place. In a nutshell, make time for making love.

Yes, sex.

Not every six months, not bimonthly, but several times a week. In the bedroom, in the basement, in the den, in the car, on the beach, on the go—the more you do it, the more you'll want to do it and the more you want to do it the more you'll actually want to be together. It may sound daunting, but what's the worst that can happen? He gets you pregnant again? Okay, so proceed with caution, but once you're well protected, throw caution to the wind!

Give it a whirl and bang like bunnies just like you did before you got married. We know you're tired, but shake it off! Shake your butt and liven up that libido. Any one of those women's magazines will tell you you're supposed to be in your sexual prime right now, so don't just sit there, do something! Buy a maid's costume, dig out your old knee socks and high school uniform—anything to get those juices flowing again.

How do you expect your marriage to feel exciting when you spend each and every night sitting on the couch watching TV and silently staring at each other during commercial breaks?

It's time to date your spouse again. It doesn't matter what you do or where you go. Just get out there and talk about something other than, "Honey, grab the Febreze, the cat puked on the wing chair again," "We need milk," or the dreaded, "You won't believe what your son did today."

All it takes is a sitter, a romantic dinner, a little wine and candlelight, and you'll both be ready for a roll in the hay, or a trip to detention, depending on whether you can still fit into that old high school uniform.

One word of caution: Look before you leap. A quick reconnaissance is always in order when you have kids. Make sure to scan the bed in case your toddler climbed in undetected during the night.

Girls' Night Out

GOD BLESS our girlfriends—swinging single, married, engaged, divorced, or desperately seeking a man. No matter what's going on in our lives, or theirs, our ladies are our life support.

Sure, it's great to spend time swapping stories about our kids and exchanging info on all our favorite mom-friendly finds. But let's face facts. Every now and then we just need a night of naughtiness and giggles with the girls.

Before you get all bent out of shape, we're not suggesting you cross the line and cheat with the chiseled jaw cutie who just bought you your third chardonnay. But who's gonna know if you have a dirty little dream about him later—we won't tell. Remember, tonight it's just us girls.

No, what we're taking about is girl's night out in its truest and purest form. Picture the scene—you and your closest girlfriends, the ones who knew you way before you were a mother, sitting in a restaurant having round after round of drinks and dish.

You rehash all of your old conquests, dream of some new ones, gossip, gab, and bridge the gap between the parents and the partiers. Tonight, it doesn't matter if you're the only one at the table with stretch marks and babies at home. Tonight, all the lines are blurred and you're once again who you were before babies and bottles came into your life. Tonight, you're just another babe in a bar.

And it feels fantastic!

Role Mommy
Reality Check

Just because you have kids doesn't mean that you can't act like a kid again. We're not saying relive all the what-was-I-thinking moments from way back when—like the time you woke up in the frat house wearing a hula skirt and wondering where you left your lei. It's just that if you don't carve out ME time and WE time while raising your kids, then you may be headed down a path that could eventually lead to the dreaded Farbissina Punim Syndrome. And trust us, once you go down that road, no one will ever want to have sex with you again, no matter what costume you wear.

OUR LIVES...
B.C. before children
and
after diapers A.D.

Confessional

B.C. When you, all sixth grade and shaky kneed, are paraded in front of the family priest, the rabbi, or your dad and forced to admit to your misdemeanor after being nabbed by a burly drugstore security guard. Your crime: pocketing a strawberry flavored Bonnie Bell lip gloss that your mom refused to buy for you.

A.D. Revealing all of your incredibly embarrassing motherhood moments to virtual strangers while anonymously blogging under the nom de plume, Mommy Dearest.."

14

Coffee Klatch Confessions

L OOK UP the word confession in the dictionary and you're likely to find a meaning like this one: *Confession: To disclose a sin you have committed or sinful thoughts in order to obtain absolution.*

Now we realize that *real* sins are the ones that require you to pull out the rosary or run straight to the rabbi in order to help you on your way to absolution and forgiveness. Sorry, we can't help you with those. That's between you and a higher power.

But, as mothers, we do know that there are other sins, the sins of motherhood, that sometimes need to be confessed along the way. That's where we come in. These aren't really sins in the traditional sense of the word. These confessionals are more like stories: those really embarrassing, sometimes horrifying, red-faced rants and recants of those maternal moments when you look around you and wonder if anyone saw what just happened. Maybe it was the time you totally messed up your daughter's class schedule and brought her to school in her Hello Kitty pajamas when Pajama Day was still a week away (every mother has her own version of this story). Or maybe it was when you planned a dinner party but had to cancel it when you were called out of town on business. You meticulously called everyone to reschedule the soiree but somehow managed to forget one name on the list. When you checked your phone messages a few hours later, you were horrified to hear from your forgotten friend, who had her husband and children in tow and just pulled up to your dark and empty house, wine bottle in hand, wondering where the hell everyone was. This actually happened to Yvette and she still can't look that friend in the eye without feeling a stabbing pang of guilt and a strong desire to run the other way.

It seems as though every mom we know these days has a confession lurking beneath that I've-got-it-all-together type A exterior. Our personal list of confessions grows with every passing day of parenthood, but here are a few doozies that we've decided to share especially with you—our new best girlfriend!

The Sassy Sinner

Yvette's Kindergarten Confessional

FORGIVE ME fellow moms, for I have sinned. Oh, it's been about five minutes since my last confession because I can't seem to go longer than that without doing something that another mom finds offensive.

It's bad when I'm out with my children and I catch another mom staring at me with her toxic judgmental dagger eyes as she happens to overhear me engaging in my two-and-a-half-year-old son's favorite new pastime called "can't say."

"Mommy," he leans in and whispers.

"Yes, Nico," I answer, bracing for what's sure to come next.

"Mommy, we can say shut down, right?"

"Yes, Nico, we can say shut down."

"But Mommy, we can't say shut up, right?"

"No, Nico, that's a bad word, we can't say that."

"And, Mommy, we can't say stupid, right? And we can't say poopy . . ." and so on and so on until he's covered every single bad word he's ever encountered—and trust me, he has quite the repertoire.

It's always fun when I hear the muffled murmurs of other moms judging my parenting skills from the sidelines.

"Oh no, she just resorted to bribery and promised her children a trip to Toys R Us if they'll sit still long enough so she can finish her glass of wine. That's a ten point parenting penalty."

"Her son just said shit and she didn't automatically put him in a time-out. I'm afraid that's an instant disqualification."

I've learned to live with it, to ignore the looks and comments and gravitate to moms whose parenting styles are similar to my own.

There's strength in numbers, girls, we've got to stick together!

But just when I thought I was immune to all the color commentary—along came the first day of kindergarten. Well, not *really* the first day of kindergarten, my husband stepped in for that one—yup, here's where I start confessing again and those other moms start judging.

Of course I wanted to be there for the first day of kindergarten, are you kidding? I'd kill for the luxury of being part of every milestone and important moment. But, like so many other moms out there, I work. My husband's schedule is far more flexible than my own so we tag team it and somehow manage to make it all happen. Dave took Christiana to school for her first week of half days and I arranged to take her in the following week for her first full day. (I never anticipated the angst involved in packing a lunch but that's another sin-filled confession that I'll get to next time.)

So, in I walked, holding my little Christiana's kindergarten hand, feeling like the mother of the year as I proudly escorted my little girl to her class, when I had the most horrific reality check of my life. The moms aren't the only ones judging me; the kids are judging me, too.

We were barely in the door when a little bratty boy announced for all to hear.

"Christiana, you're late. Why did your Mommy bring you to school late? You already missed announcements." We were, like, two minutes late. Come on, parking's a bitch, kid!

And if that wasn't bad enough, another little Judge Judy in the making chimed in.

"Are you Christiana's Mommy? We've never seen you here before. Where have you been?"

Uh, how about at work, using my brain and making sure my daughter has a successful, accomplished role model to look up to so she can always be reminded that she can accomplish anything she sets her mind to? But, that doesn't seem to matter when your kindergartener wants to fit in with all the other kids in the class.

So, I've made a vow to repent, show up at school on time, and make sure I leave little love notes in Christiana's lunch so she can be like all the rest of the kids who literally compare notes on how much their mommies love them.

I made a vow to be a prompt parent, but once a sinner, always a sinner.

Keep right on judging me ladies, gentlemen, and now, kiddies, too, but I never will issue a time-out when Christiana slips and says a bad word. After all, guess who she probably heard it from?

Yup, I may always be a sinner, but I'll never be a hypocrite.

The Playground Pariah

Beth's Story

I HATE playgrounds. I don't like sandboxes, either, have never been able to swing from the monkey bars, and pretty much cringe when my kids insist we go to the park on an unusually brisk day even though they can entertain themselves to their hearts' content with the swing set and seven-foot-high climbing structure that lays barren and unused (except by squirrels and spiders) in our lonely backyard.

I know, I sound like a big old sourpuss. But I am not alone. My good friend Alicia hates playgrounds, too. She's always on edge whenever our kids drag us there—afraid she'll lose track of her son or concerned he'll get pummeled by a kid wielding a plastic shovel.

In my years of circumventing the playground circuit, I've found they are a haven for serial playdaters, bullies, new moms angling for adult attention, nanny cliques, and pets without leashes. Personally, I prefer to take the fun indoors, where I know my kid won't race off at a moment's notice when the ice cream man starts ringing that incessant Pavlovian bell that sends scores of kids clamoring for a drippy ice cream pop that resembles Sponge Bob on a really bad day.

And what about that sand box? If the kids have driven you stir crazy on a rainy afternoon and you agree to take them to the playground once the downpour finally stops, you'll find the sand box reduced to a mud pit that invariably winds up tracked into your hall with filthy Stride Rites that are in desperate need of the spin cycle. On unusually hot days, toddlers can be seen running for dear life when their little tootsies are scorched the moment they hit the molten pit. On decent weather days, the sand box is a haven for kids using Tonka dump trucks and shovels that they can swing in all directions, flinging sand high into the air that lands smack into the eyes and mouth of an unsuspecting two-year-old.

Let's not forget about the swings. Swings can actually be fun—except, somehow, they've made them much narrower than my protruding posterior can handle. And so, when my daughter and I set off on a swing race—whoever swings highest wins—my corpulent bottom usually holds me back as she soars toward the top rung of that shaky metal swing set.

As for the monkey bars—they are not even an option for me. I have a hard enough time doing push-ups, much less attempting to yank myself from one bar to the next. All I can do is stand underneath my kids, who effortlessly swing themselves across as I watch in amazement wondering if I ever did that in my life. The answer—nope, the only bars I've tackled in my lifetime were the ones that sold watered down woo woos and cosmopolitans, and personally, I'd prefer to keep it that way.

I know I sound like a party pooper—what kind of parent doesn't like to take their kids to the park for an afternoon of frolicking and fun? But for me, I love finding things that I can do with them where I can enjoy myself too.

First activity—manicures. I've taken my daughter to our local nail salon since she was two years old; in fact, all the manicure ladies know her by name and ask about her whenever I sneak out of the house without her for some me time. I know, a kiddy manicure may seem a little overindulgent, but guess what? When she's an adult, she'll already be a pro at carving out me time, and maybe when I'm bunking at an assisted living facility, she'll break me out and invite me along for a spa day.

Then there's ice skating. There is nothing like spending an hour at the ice rink with my daughter, who eagerly races onto the ice every Sunday for her figure skating lessons. While she learns how to master her spins and skate backwards, I get to strap on my skates and listen to Casey Kasem's top 40 from the

1980s—I can't think of a better experience than that!

Or, now here's a concept, what if our kids went to play with their own friends and we didn't monitor their every move? When I was a little kid, my mom would let my brother and me venture outside and play with our friends, and we would disappear for hours on end. We played dodge ball, built tree houses, smoked cigarettes when we were only six years old, got caught shoplifting at seven . . . okay, maybe it wasn't such a good idea to let us roam free after all. But I digress.

These days my kids pretty much can only play where we can see them. Want to ride your bike? Well, Daddy will be jogging alongside you then. Want to walk to school by yourself? Not on your life. Want to play with your little friend up in your bedroom with the door closed? Think again. That door had better stay open, and I'm switching on the baby monitor to make sure nothing dangerous goes on in there.

As for the park—as much as I dread going there, it's still a prime destination that my kids treasure visiting all year round. Lucky

for me, my husband takes charge and takes
them to the playground while I putter around
the house, run errands, and sometimes even
attempt to cook a decent meal for our family
—oh, who are we kidding, I also slip out
to do some serious damage at Ann Taylor
Loft.

I Bribe, Therefore I Am

Beth's Story

IF THE Supernanny ever paid a visit to the
Feldman homestead, she'd definitely be
giving me that tsk tsk look when it comes to
my parenting style. You see, when my kids
whine to get their way, or repeat themselves
at least a dozen times asking for the same
damn thing over and over and over again, I
pretty much flip off the switch in my brain
and enter into bribery mode.

I have found that a good old fashioned cash
bribe can ward off everything from nagging to
fighting with siblings to repetitive questioning
by a preschooler. In fact, I've even dangled a
five spot in front of my son to prevent him
from spilling the beans on a surprise party for

a good friend of mine. And guess what? The bribe worked! He kept his trap shut and the surprise went off without a hitch.

Bribery can take on many forms. I've been known to tempt my kids with ice cream, sugary sweets, prizes from long forgotten birthday goody bags, and if I'm really under pressure, a limited edition Webkinz that can only be found on eBay. If a little reward for good behavior will translate into peace and quiet on the home front, I say, what's the big deal? People get bonuses at work. Why shouldn't our kids get bonuses when they do the right thing?

Although it seems my kids could be destined for a lifetime of bratty behavior with my bribery tactics, I say my ingenious reward system is achieving quite the contrary. My kids know full well that bad behavior will not be rewarded, but if they both participate in a who-can-fold-the-laundry-fastest contest, the payoff might just be a trip to the supermarket, where they can each select their favorite box of cereal that comes complete with a plastic pedometer they'll both treasure for at least the next hour or two.

So if Jo Frost, the infamous Supernanny, spent a few weeks observing my parenting skills, would I fail miserably with my ruthless bribery tactics? Probably, but all I can say is that if no one is fighting, they've finished their homework, and put away all their toys, what's a little tchotchke or piece of candy to make their day . . . and mine!

Why I Don't Send Holiday Cards
A Feldman Family Tradition

I'M CONVINCED it must have started with my wedding. We had about 300 partygoers for our blowout celebration at a synagogue that reminded me of that cathedral where Maria from the *Sound of Music* got married. We then jetted off for a romantic honeymoon in Italy and returned home three weeks later to start our lives together as a married couple—with shared responsibilities, combined checking accounts, and thoughts of babies dancing in my head.

In lieu of being carried over the threshold, I dragged my steamer trunk back into our gift-wrap-strewn apartment and was immediately awoken from my jet-lag-induced haze when I realized that I would be put in charge of writing out all the thank you cards to our wonderful guests.

At first I really made an effort to be gracious to our friends, loved ones, and perfect strangers. "Thank you for your generous gift. We were so happy you could share our special day with us, blah bidi blah blah blah," but after about thirty cards, my hand started hurting and I stopped. Forever.

When my kids were born, I tried the thank you card route once again but pretty much dropped out as soon as I started. "Thanks for the pink satin onesie, it was soooooooooo cute!" Again, after about twenty thank yous, I gave up my gratitude mission and moved onto something more productive, like operating the TV remote control while breastfeeding. Once in a while I'd get a message from someone who had sent a gift but never got back a thank you card. "Did you get my present? I hadn't heard from you so I was hoping you received it." Yes, I got it. I'm just too damn lazy to send a card back to thank you, but now that you're calling, hey, thanks for the gift, I always wanted a bottle warmer.

And then, as my kids got older, we started to receive them. Every year, like clockwork they'd wind up in our mailbox. You know what I'm talking about: the dreaded holiday photo cards. Greetings from the Ignazios, Love and kisses from the Kleins, Shalom from the Lichtinsteins—what's missing from this illustrustious bunch? You guessed it, a happy-go-lucky pose from the hapless Feldmans.

At first, we figured, we're Jewish, we're off the hook. Who sends a photo card to wish their friends Happy Hannukah or Belated Yom Kippur Greetings anyway? It seemed a little weird to gather round and strike a pose in the name of Judaism, so we shrugged it off and went on our merry way. But then, the cards kept on coming. And they started to increase in their intensity—Ni hao from the Changs, Happy Kwanza from the Martins, Greetings from Archie (my girlfriend's Labrador Retriever).

Every time we'd open the mailbox, there would be another batch of smiling faces that I didn't recognize because either I hadn't seen my friend in years or my husband's clients decided to add us to their holiday mailing list.

Now, honestly, if I don't know who you are, do you really think I'm going to care when you send me a picture of your blond-haired blue-eyed pixies sitting atop Santa's lap? Let's be real, I could be watching a Sears commercial and it would elicit the same reaction.

When we'd visit someone's house during the fall or winter months, they'd have their refrigerators adorned with holiday photos from their friends and loved ones and then they'd say to us, "Where are your photos? We've never once received a holiday card from you." When my kids were too young to answer for us, I'd just reply that if my friends wanted to know what my children looked like, they were welcome to come over any time. But then, when my own children started catching on and realized we never pose for holiday shots, they got in on the act too.

"Mommy, why don't we have holiday cards with our photo on it?"

"Because we don't celebrate Christmas, sweetie, that's why."

"But the Goldbergs just sent us a photo of their family around their Hannukah bush. Why can't we do that?"

"Because we don't have a bush, we only have a menorah, and, oh, we just don't do it because we're taking a stand and saving trees."

"Well, we should take a photo and send out a holiday card, Mom. Everybody else does it."

And so, just because everybody else does it, do the Feldmans have to join the insanity and dress everybody up in August to make it look like its winter? And even more frustrating, am I the one who has to compile the mailing list and figure out how to merge the addresses into labels and then head to the post office so I can buy a cute collection of holiday stamps and then send it out to all our friends? I say, no way.

Besides, I have earned quite the reputation as the one who never sends thank yous for anything—I've moved on from my wedding to my kids' birth announcements to birthdays to anniversaries. In fact, if Emily Post were alive, she'd probably keel over when she learned that I pretty much have ignored every etiquette rule in the book involving thank you and holiday correspondence.

I've narrowly squeaked by over the last decade offering excuse after excuse about why I never send thank you and holiday cards, but it appears as if technology may have gotten the best of me. I can take a picture, send it to a Web site, and then email it out to all my nearest and dearest friends. Maybe now that it's so easy, I'll actually sift through all the photos that I've uploaded to my computer but have never printed out and create an unforgettable holiday masterpiece.

Then again, maybe not.

Role Mommy
Reality Check

It doesn't matter if you hate playgrounds, don't send holiday cards, openly bribe your kids with ring pops and Webkinz, or teach your kids to curse like sailors. No matter your religion or ethnic persuasion, a good old confession is always good for the soul. And isn't it much more fun to share your innermost transgressions with your closest confidantes or those mixed up mommies in cyberspace? After all, a good girlfriend will always forgive you for your sins.

15

The Official Role
Mommy Wish List

*Mandatory office hours for all pediatricians
—from 6 a.m. to 8 p.m.

DON'T WE have enough to worry about when our children are sick and we are stuck at the office worrying about them? We get so stressed out over how we're going to get our kids to the doctors that we end up speeding through traffic with a migraine and an ulcer eating away at our stomachs. By the time we get to the doctor, we're sicker than our kids and need a doctor's appointment ourselves. Yeah, like that will ever happen.

Beth's been walking around with the same sinus infection since 2004.

*Fewer homework hassles

WE'VE BEEN stuck behind a desk at work and away from our kids all day. Now, we're home and finally able to spend some time with them. Do we really want to spend the remainder of our evening trying to figure out how long it will take two men, who have capsized in a boat 30 miles from shore, swimming three miles an hour to make it to land?

*Stores will sell winter clothes during the winter months and summer clothes during the summer months.

BUSY MOMS live in the moment. We don't want to worry about Halloween costumes in August or swimsuits in December. We can't work that far ahead. It makes us crazy when we walk into a store in July, in search of a cute little size 6X bikini, only to be greeted with aisles and aisles of snowsuits. And, of course, when we're ready to buy those snowsuits, they're long gone and our husbands want to kill us because we've stuck our son in an adorable pink bunny parka that his sister grew out of two years ago.

Parents will stop competing against each other to see who can throw the most extravagant children's party.

ENOUGH ALREADY. Is it really necessary to rent out the entire amusement park and have pony rides, a jumping castle, petting zoo, face painting, and yes, even a parade of princesses for your preschooler's party? We know you want to one-up your neighbor who had a hoe-down complete with a kids rodeo in his backyard last year, but it's time to stop the insanity. The same people who spend thousands on these kid parties are the same ones who are up all night wondering how they're going to pay for college. Stop throwing ridiculous kid parties, that's how. And when it comes to goody bags, please have a little restraint. Our kids have enough crap at home already, thank you. We don't need a suitcase-sized sack filled with more crap. A simple small bag with some good old fashioned teeth-rotting candy will be just fine.

*Doctors will create a vaccine for moaning and whining.

IF THEY can figure out a way to protect us from things like chicken pox and the flu, why not eradicate the two things that seem to sicken parents on a daily basis?

*Scientists will create a magnetic microchip that will instantly plop your child's posterior into their car seat.

THINK ABOUT all the time you waste begging, bargaining, and bribing your children to sit in their car seats. How great would it be to have a little magnetic device in your baby's butt that instantly seals them in their seat the moment they get in the car.

*Our kids will be content to wear exactly what we pick out for them for school.

WE KNOW you've been there. You've got 20 minutes to throw the kids into their school clothes and you find yourself rummaging through fifteen pairs of pants that they refuse to wear because each one doesn't quite fit to their specifications. Then, after you attempt to put on their socks, they complain that the seam in the front is tugging at their pinky toe. Enough of this Princess/Prince and the Pea mentality. Wear what we tell you to wear or you can prance into preschool in your Scooby Doo pajamas.

OUR LIVES...
B.C. before children
and
after diapers A.D.

Happy Hour

B.C. Those wonderful twilight after-work hours spent socializing and sharing cocktails with your friends and colleagues—the trendier the bar the better.

A.D. Those precious 60 minutes of solitude at the end of your marathon day (usually around 10 or 11 p.m.) when your work is done—emails responded to, BlackBerry put away, kitchen Swiffered, dishwasher loaded, homework done, kids asleep, lunches packed for the next day, laundry folded —and you can finally collapse on the couch with a cocktail and some really bad TV before you go to bed and get up at 6 a.m. to do it all over again.

Acknowledgments

Where do we even begin? We have tons of people to thank for putting up with us during this incredibly circuitous journey. Thanks to our friends, family, and perfect strangers who read our stories, laughed along, and encouraged us to keep on going!

To our husbands—Darin and Dave—for being our biggest cheerleaders and reading and rereading every single rewrite and revision and, most importantly, entertaining the troops while we hid out in Beth's bat cave.

To our parents—Neil and Lenore and Kiki and Tasso—for showing us what a difference a wonderful childhood can make and for teaching us to laugh at life and appreciate all the milestones.

To Darin's mom, Sally, and step-dad, John, for giving Beth plenty of comedic inspiration.

To Dave's parents, Jack and Harriett, for the endless games of Hide and Seek so Yvette could actually get some work done.

Nick Katsoris and NK Publications, you are the dream maker—thanks for making it all come true.

Dorothy Weber—for taking a leap of faith and believing in two women with big dreams and big mouths.

Lauren Petterson—for giving us a chance and opening so many doors. Now, let's talk about hair and makeup!

Marie Hickey—for putting up with Yvette for so many years and proving to us every day that you can be a great mom and have an amazing career.

Lisa Gregorisch and Theresa Coffino—for giving Yvette a wonderful reason to return to work and for making every day an excellent adventure.

Emily Francis and Sukanya Krishnan—for rockin' those Role Mommy T-shirts.

Chris Ender and Gil Schwartz—for taking a chance on Beth and giving her the opportunity to soar.

Jeremy Murphy—for being the best book editor money can't buy.

To our fabulous editor, Shana Drehs, for guidance, support, and above all, getting it!

Debbie Marcus—for being an amazing radio producer and a really great friend.

The CBS Communications and Marketing team—for offering encouragement, amazing ideas, advice, and lots of great stories.

Michael Starr—our favorite *NY Post* columnist and cheerleader.

Tanika Ray, Mera Lome, and Yvette's amazing friends at *Extra*—for sharing so many laughs as well as your rolodexes.

Carolina Buia—for all of the great advice and insight.

Margaret Gleason—for giving our book heart.

Jeanne Fitzmaurice, Sue McMillan, Esther Luc, and the Design-her Gals team—for giving us a purpose as well as a really cool cover.

Robin, Susan, Mei Mei, Erica, Lauren, Olga, Endria, Adrianna, and Karen for being the best coffee klatch on the planet!

Carolina Manero for our fabulous photo shoot.

Sue Kupcinet—for reading and helping us edit our manuscript and for being one of our biggest cheerleaders!

Beth Davis—for being an amazing friend and future Role Mommy!

Amy Collins—for taking it upon herself to take us to the next step.

Our incredible literary agent Carol Mann—who believed in our project, found it the perfect home, and made our dream come true!

Sabrina Weill—for your continued support and for connecting us with the amazing Carol Mann!

Yvette's aunts: Demi, Maria, Nitsa, Dorothy, and Agatha—for proving that aunts are Role Mommies, too, and that Greek goddesses do exist.

Beth's Grandmothers Dora and Dora—for passing on the mean matzoh ball soup gene, as well as the witty sarcasm that seeped its way into every page of this book!

About the Authors

Photo by Carolina Manero

BY DAY, they're the dynamic duo of broadcast bookings. By night—after the kids are in bed and the dishwasher is loaded—they're the cocreators of Role Mommy.

Our story begins in 1998 when Yvette Manessis Corporon (left, above) and Beth Feldman were making their mark on the television industry—Yvette as an adrenaline-addicted Emmy Award–winning news producer for New York's WCBS-TV and Beth as an entertainment publicist for the CBS Television Network.

Married, but without kids, the two first became fast friends while coordinating appearances by some of the brightest stars in the CBS line-up, as well as some of the dullest wanna-be A-listers who never did make it past D-list status. Yvette and Beth were each other's go-to gals, always coming through in a pinch when one needed a "get" in order to score some much-needed points with her boss.

Fast forward to 2004. Yvette, who has had two children and taken a hiatus from full-time work, has rejoined the workforce as a producer for the television show *Extra*. She's traded in the seductive siren call of the news-room for sit-down celebrity interviews and given up all-night undercover investigative work in order to slip under the covers and cuddle with her kids at bedtime. Beth, who has since had two children and never left the workforce, has clawed her way up the corpo-rate ladder and has graduated from promoting one-season series, such as *Welcome to New York* and *Dellaventura*, to handling hits such as *Everybody Loves Raymond*, *The Amazing Race*, and *CSI*.

Together, Yvette and Beth reconnected and never missed a beat. With camera crews trailing behind, they have traipsed across the streets of New York with just about every television star you can imagine, and some they'd rather forget. While coordinating red carpet events, elaborate junkets, and exclusive backstage set visits, the two women forged a professional and personal bond as they swapped stories about their chaotic careers, expanding families, and ever-fading free time.

It was only a matter of time until, as frenzied friends meeting over a chicken-salad-with-dressing-on-the-side lunch, they discovered they were each other's Role Mommy. An idea was hatched and a book was born. Individually they've balanced bookings, bottles, conference calls, and croup—and together, they embarked on a new journey. Without the aid of modern science or even leaving their husbands, these two women gave birth to *Peeing in Peace* and the Role Mommy brand.

Since it's inception in 2005, the Role Mommy movement has spread like wildfire.

Role Mommy joined forces with the Children's Museum of Manhattan and the Westchester County Parks Department and launched a highly successful lecture series featuring successful women who have reinvented their lives while raising a family. The popular panel discussions have featured celebrated and celebrity working mothers, such as Kassie DePaiva (*One Life to Live*), Barbara Corcoran (real estate goddess), Rene Syler (*The Early Show*), Martha Byrne (*As The World Turns*), Pilar Guzman (editor-in-chief of *Cookie Magazine*), Lisa Caputo (president of Women and Company for Citigroup and former press secretary to Hillary Clinton during the Clinton White House years), Lee Woodruff (best-selling author, *In An Instant*), and Cindy Hsu (television news reporter with WCBS-TV in New York).

Yvette and Beth have also moved out from behind the cameras and into the hair and makeup chair and have appeared as parenting contributors on the CW11 *Morning News* in New York, and have also been featured on Fox News Channels' *FOX & Friends*, iVillage Live, WCBS-TV, and FOX 5 NY, as well as radio stations nationwide, sharing their stories, sagas, and sometimes silliness of their lives as working mothers. Beth is also a regular contributor to *New York Metroparents*, *Hybrid Mom*, *Time Out New York Kids*, *Westchester Family*, and the *Huffington Post*, among others.

Whereas Yvette continues her ascent up the entertainment ladder and is now a senior segment producer at *Extra*, Beth has pole-vaulted off her perch at CBS to embark on a brand new venture, launching BeyondPR —an entertainment public relations and talent consulting firm representing television projects, innovative Web sites, and best-selling authors. She also continues to be the driving force behind Role Mommy, where she produces events for parents and writes and manages all of the content for the popular Role Mommy website. Rolemommy.com has become an online coffee klatch where busy moms can log in and get a quick fix of camara-derie and a laugh before getting on with their busy lives. The mission of Role Mommy is simple: to inspire and entertain.

ABOUT DESIGN-HER GALS

Design-her Gals (www.designhergals.com) is a fun, interactive web-based company that allows women to create their virtual self by selecting skin tone, eye color, and hair style and color, as well as choosing from hundreds of outfits and accessories and having your "gal" produced into an assortment of personalized stationery products and other clothing and gift items. The passion and purpose of Design-her Gals is to raise funds and awareness for stage IV breast cancer patients through its nonprofit sister organization, the Gal to Gal Foundation. A portion of all proceeds from Design-her Gals goes toward this important cause.

The Gal to Gal Foundation believes that women diagnosed with stage IV breast cancer deserve a great amount of support in order to maintain their dignity while receiving treatment throughout the progression of their disease. Over three hundred thousand patients worldwide will lose their lives to stage IV breast cancer this year. The Gal to Gal Foundation identifies, partners with, and provides funding to existing organizations dedicated to the emotional and financial well-being of stage IV breast cancer survivors.

Design-her Gals has enjoyed consistent press coverage and celebrity endorsements. This year, Design-her Gals was highlighted in *O Magazine* as one of Oprah Winfrey's "O List of Favorite Things." Oprah called the site "ridiculously addictive." Many television, radio, and print media have promoted the site, including the *Martha Stewart Show*, the *TODAY* show, Lifetime Television for Women, AM Northwest, *The Daily Buzz*, businessweek.com, mommycast (podcast), *The New York Post*, the *Chicago Tribune*, the *San Diego Union Tribune*, *Woman's Day*, *Life & Style*, *Modern Bride*, *Teen Magazine*, *In Touch Weekly*, and many more.

Design-her Gals is a virtual company with a servicing and design team of "gal pals" throughout the United States (many are type A moms!) dedicating themselves to a "high-tech/high-touch" customer service approach to their fast-growing community. Design-her Gals has a strong management team in place, led by Jeanne K. Fitzmaurice, who possesses more than twenty-five years of business experience and is an award-winning leader and innovator recognized for her strategic expertise. Jeanne is a frequent speaker at conferences related to Internet marketing and female entrepreneurs.